Faith That Moves Mountains

Developing Unwavering Faith

Gary Ward

Copyright © 2011 by Gary Ward

All rights reserved. No part of this book may be used, reproduced, stored in a retrieval system, or transmitted in any form whatsoever — including electronic, photocopy, recording — without prior written permission from the author, except in the case of brief quotations embodied in critical articles or reviews.

Scripture quotations, unless otherwise stated, are taken from the *New American Standard Bible.* Copyright © 1960, 1962, 1963, 1968, 1971, 1972, 1973, 1975, 1977, 1995 by The Lockman Foundation. All rights reserved.

FIRST EDITION

ISBN: 9780982947678

Library of Congress Control Number: 2011922908

Published by
NewBookPublishing.com, a division of Reliance Media, Inc.
2395 Apopka Blvd., #200, Apopka, FL 32703
NewBookPublishing.com

Printed in the United States of America

Reliance Media

Table Of Contents

	Introduction	5
1	Overcoming, Mountain-Moving Faith: An Overview	7
2	The Eyes Of Your Heart, The Eyes Of Faith	17
3	Faith Works	25
4	Faith Under Pressure	31
5	Faith And The Storms Of Life	41
6	Ever-Enlarging Faith	51
7	The Testing Of Our Faith	59
8	Faith And Patience	67
9	Hindrances To Faith	75
10	Faith And The Impossible	83
11	Signs And Wonders And Faith	91
12	Faith And Thanksgiving	99
13	Faith And Healing	105
14	Contending Earnestly For The Faith	117
15	Leaving A Legacy Of Faith	125
	About The Author	127

Introduction

Faith. Much has already been written about faith. Why another book?

This one is different. It takes a look at faith from a biblical perspective, looking at faith as God sees it, according to His word.

This book includes only a few contemporary examples of faith working in peoples' lives. That is intentional so that your faith is founded on the word of God. "...that your faith should not rest on the wisdom of men, but on the power of God" (1 Corinthians 2:5).

As you read through the various aspects of faith, you will find your own faith being greatly enlarged and more effective. Our goal is to develop our faith to the place it is, as the Scripture says, "overcoming, mountain-moving" faith.

This book is based on the premise that Bible faith always works. We all have at one time or another thought we were in faith, but it did not seem to bring the results we hoped for. Too often we wrongly concluded then, that faith does not work. Later we realized we were not really in faith as described clearly in the Scriptures.

Fear, the opposite of faith, can sometimes look like faith. Hope may be confused with faith. Learn what real Bible faith is and how it is instrumental in receiving the promises and blessings of God.

"Now faith is the assurance of things hoped for, the conviction of things not seen" (Hebrews 11:1).

Chapter 1

❖ ❖ ❖

Overcoming, Mountian-Moving Faith: An Overview

"And Jesus answered saying to them, 'Have faith in God. Truly I say to you, whoever says to this mountain, "Be taken up and cast into the sea," and does not doubt in his heart, but believes that what he says is going to happen, it shall be granted him. Therefore I say to you, all things for which you pray and ask, believe that you have received them, and they shall be granted you'" (Mark 11:22-24).

"For whatever is born of God overcomes the world; and this is the victory that has overcome the world - our faith" (1 John 5:4).

What is Faith?

What is this overcoming, mountain-moving faith? The dictionary defines faith as: "unquestioning belief, complete trust, confidence, reliance on."

But what does God's word (the Bible) say about what

faith is, what it can do, how we receive and develop it, and what we do with it in difficult times? These are only a few of the things that are included in this book.

In this chapter we will take an overview to give you an idea of what is ahead. We begin by stating what faith is not. Faith is *not* a religion, a movement, a camp, or a trendy doctrine.

It is believing with absolute, unwavering trust and confidence in God's word. It is a dynamic and powerful force, a style of life we are to live. The Bible says repeatedly that the righteous person shall live by faith. See Habakkuk 2:4, Galatians 3:11, Hebrews 10:38, and Romans 1:17.

The Bible defines faith very precisely. Even though various versions and translations use different wording, the meaning comes through clearly in each one.

Hebrews 11:1 is where we find the definition. Following are several ways it has been translated or paraphrased.

NAS "Now faith is the assurance of things hoped for, the conviction of things not seen."

NIV "Now faith is being sure of what we hope for and certain of what we do not see."

KJ "Now faith is the substance of things hoped for, the evidence of things not seen."

Amplified Bible "Now faith is the assurance (the confirmation, the title-deed) of the things we hope for, being the proof of things we do not see and the conviction of their reality - faith perceiving as real fact what is not revealed to the senses."

NEB "And what is faith? Faith gives substance to our hopes and makes us certain of realities we do not see."

TLB "What is faith? It is the confident assurance that something we want is going to happen. It is the certainty that what we hope for is waiting for us, even though we cannot see it up ahead."

GWB "Faith assures us of things we expect and convinces us of the existence of things we cannot see."

Notice that the wording above includes "assurance, conviction, sure, certain, substance, evidence, confirmation, title-deed, confident," and "expect."

Faith and the Word of God

Faith was born of God and was working in the Garden of Eden. God told Adam and Eve to enjoy all the trees but one, the knowledge of good and evil. He said if you eat of it, you will surely die.

"Then the Lord God took the man and put him into the Garden of Eden to cultivate it and keep it. And the Lord God commanded the man, saying, 'From any tree of the garden you may eat freely; but from the tree of the knowledge of good and evil you shall not eat, for in the day that you eat from it you shall surely die'" (Genesis 2:15-17).

Satan came to steal that word of God from them. He

came to get them off the word of God, to get them into doubt, to do whatever he could do so they wouldn't stay on God's word. He will do the same to you.

Satan told them, "You won't surely die." He was trying to convince Adam and Eve that God's word isn't for sure, it's not certain, it's not absolute. God is just trying to prevent you from having a good time.

You must not let your adversary take you away from God's word! Why is that important? Because, as we will see later, *faith must always be based on God's word*, either His spoken word or His written word. There will be more on this in a later chapter.

"For indeed we have had good news preached to us, just as they also; but the word they heard did not profit them, because it was not united by faith in those who heard" (Hebrews 4:2).

As we proceed with developing an understanding of faith, keep in mind that it is born of God. He created it. He is the author of it. Faith is His idea and it is for your benefit.

"Fixing your eyes on Jesus, the author & perfecter of faith" (Hebrews 12:2).

"Whatever is born of God overcomes. This is what overcomes the world - our faith" (1 John 5:4).

Faith is born of God. Faith is birthed in us at our new birth, when we are born again. Romans 12:3 tells us, "God has allotted to each a measure of faith."

We can develop and strengthen it, or neglect and lose it altogether.

Developing Faith

Faith can be developed and strengthened, or it can atrophy through lack of use, like muscles do. You may have walked in strong faith once but have allowed it to deteriorate and become ineffective through lack of use.

It is important to understand faith: what it is, how it works effectively, and what hinders its effectiveness.

Again, different versions express the thought differently, but all say the same thing. In 2 Thessalonians 1:3-4, we read, "Faith is greatly enlarged" (NAS),

"Faith is growing more & more" (NIV), and "Faith groweth exceedingly" (KJ).

The Greek language here is strong: "to increase beyond measure; greatly enlarged."

With that in mind, look at a few other ways this growth and strengthening of our faith is described.

GWB "your faith is showing remarkable growth"

NEB "your faith increases mightily"

The Message "faith is growing phenomenally"

CEV "faith keeps growing all the time."

So, we receive a measure of faith when we are born

again; then we must develop it into effectiveness. It is a lifetime process of continual growth.

Faith is not automatic. You will start with faith at your new birth, but must develop it to make it strong.

Everything must be maintained if it is to last. That includes our faith.

Maintaining Your Faith

In the last days some will fall away from faith. "But the Spirit explicitly says that in later times some will fall away from the faith, paying attention to deceitful spirits and doctrines of demons..." (1Timothy 4:1).

Others will shipwreck in regard to their faith, broken up by storms of life. "...keeping faith and a good conscience, which some have rejected and suffered shipwreck in regard to their faith" (1Timothy 1:19).

You may be in faith today. Will you be in tomorrow? Will you remain strong in faith when storms hit? Will you be in faith when the pressures of life set in? It depends largely on what you are doing with your faith today.

You can build your muscles to be strong, and then quit exercising. No matter how strong you were, you will atrophy. After awhile it was as if you had not been strong at all. It is the same with your faith. What are you doing with your faith today?

As you read on about faith and see how it can be

strengthened and become more effective, I believe your faith will grow stronger.

Holding on to Your Faith

Staying in faith is not automatic. You can lose it, draw back from it, shipwreck, or let your adversary take it from you. That is why the Bible says you must contend for your faith. You must fight for it. You must hang on to it and do not let go.

"...contend earnestly for the faith..." (Jude 3).

You have an adversary who would destroy the effectiveness of your faith, seduce you, draw you away from it, and get you to doubt God's word. Later, you will find a chapter helping you to know how to hang onto your faith and not lose it.

Moving Mountains

Let's go back to Mark 11:22-24 for just a moment and look at one more thing. It is important to note that the word "mountain" can be used literally or figuratively in the Bible.

Mountain is defined as follows: "To rise up or rear up as a mountain. Lifting itself above the plain."

"Mountain moving" is often used in speaking of overcoming difficulties or accomplishing great things. In the great love chapter (1 Corinthians 13:2), we read, "If I have all faith so as to move mountains..."

The psalmist in Psalm 3:1 says, "O Lord, how my adversaries have increased! Many are rising up against me."

In Matthew 17, we read an account of a father who brought his demon-possessed son to the disciples for deliverance. They could not cast the demon out, and later they asked Jesus why they were ineffective at setting the boy free.

Jesus' answer as recorded in the Amplified Bible was, "He said to them, 'Because of the littleness of your faith - that is, your lack of firmly relying trust. For truly, I say to you, if you have faith (that is living) like a grain of mustard seed, you can say to this mountain, move from here to yonder place, and it will move, and nothing will be impossible to you'" (Matthew 17:20).

Absolute Faith

Faith is the conviction, the absolute trust in, the assurance of that which is hoped for in the word of God, knowing that it is true and that it will be manifested into substance, reality, in our life.

There is to be no argument, no doubt, no debate, and no hesitation regarding the truth of God's word.

"If any of you lacks wisdom, let him ask of God, who gives to all men generously and without reproach, and it will be given to him. But let him ask in faith without any doubting, for the one who doubts is like the surf of the sea, driven and tossed by the wind. For let not that man expect that he will receive anything from the Lord, being a double-minded man, unstable in all his ways" (James 1:5-8).

Faith and Opposing Circumstances

"And in the fourth watch of the night He came to them, walking on the sea. When the disciples saw Him walking on the sea, they were terrified, and said, 'It is a ghost!' And they cried out in fear. But immediately Jesus spoke to them, saying, 'Take courage, it is I; do not be afraid.' Peter said to Him, 'Lord, if it is You, command me to come to You on the water.' And He said, 'Come!' And Peter got out of the boat, and walked on the water and came toward Jesus. But seeing the wind, he became frightened, and beginning to sink, he cried out, 'Lord, save me!' Immediately Jesus stretched out His hand and took hold of him, and said to him, 'You of little faith, why did you doubt?'" (Matthew 14:25-31).

For awhile, faith overcame fear. For awhile, Peter had his eyes fixed on Jesus and was responding to His word. As long as he did that, Peter walked in the supernatural. It was when he took his eyes off Jesus and looked around at the circumstances, which spoke against his ability to walk on water, that he sank. Jesus rebuked him for his little faith.

As you go through this book, you will find that the principles pointed out in this chapter will be built upon and expanded. Enjoy your adventure in learning about real, Bible faith! Learn how to develop overcoming, mountain-moving faith and move into the supernatural realm.

NAS New American Standard

NIV New International Version

KJ King James

NEB New English Bible

TLB The Living Bible

GWB God's Word Bible

CEV Contemporary English Version

Chapter 2

❖ ❖ ❖

The Eyes Of Your Heart, The Eyes Of Faith

When surrounded by a multitude of the enemy forces, Elisha's servant was fearful. "Now when the attendant of the man of God had risen early and gone out, behold an army with horses and chariots was encircling the city. And his servant said to him, 'Alas, my master! What shall we do?'" (2 Kings 6:15).

That is a common response of people today when surrounded by trouble.

Elisha replied to the servant with what must have seemed like an odd statement: "Do not fear, for those who are with us are more than those who are with them" (2 Kings 6:16).

Elisha must have been seeing something his servant could not see. Recognizing that the servant was fearful of what he saw, Elisha prayed, "and said, 'O Lord, I pray, open his eyes that he may see.' And the Lord opened the servant's eyes and he saw; and behold, the mountain was full of horses and chariots of fire all around Elisha" (2 Kings 6:17).

We have two sets of eyes by which we may see. Natural eyes see things in the natural realm; spiritual eyes see by faith into the spiritual realm.

Remember: Faith has to do with bringing things into manifestation in the seen, natural realm from the unseen, spiritual realm. "Now faith is the assurance of things hoped for, the conviction of things *not seen*" (Hebrews 11:1).

Walking by Faith, Not by Sight

Apostle Paul put it this way: "We walk by faith, not by sight" (2 Corinthians 5:7). He said, "I pray that the eyes of your heart be enlightened, so that you will know what is the hope of His calling, what are the riches of the glory of His inheritance in the saints, and what is the surpassing greatness of His power toward us who believe. These are in accordance with the working of the strength of His might..." (Ephesians 1:18-19).

Faith requires enlightenment of our spiritual eyes so that we might see the promises of God as reality in our lives. God's word enlightens us regarding the unseen things of the spiritual realm.

Natural sight does not see the same things as spiritual eyes do. Which then do we use? Both; but spiritual eyes should determine how we live.

"The righteous shall live by faith" (Habakkuk 2:4). This is confirmed three times in the New Testament as noted in the first chapter.

What did They See?

Although many biblical accounts clearly illustrate the conflict that can arise between the input from these two sets of eyes, none does it better than what is recorded in the book of Numbers, Chapters 13 and 14.

God told Moses to send spies into the Promised Land, to scout it out, and bring back a report to the people. He said that He was going to give the land to them (Numbers 13:2). So Moses sent out the spies with instructions to go see what they could and come back and tell the people about it (vs. 17-20).

The spies looked things over and came back with their report of what they had seen (vs. 21-26). At first they confirmed what God had told them, that the land was in fact flowing with milk and honey, and with great fruit (vs. 27). But then, they said, "nevertheless..."

Do Not Add to God's Word

Let us pause here to see what was about to happen, because it is instructional for us today. A very important principle from God's word is about to be violated.

"Every word of God is tested; He is a shield to those who take refuge in Him. Do not add to His words or He will reprove you and you will be proved a liar" (Proverbs 30:5).

Do not add to God's word. The most common way we add to His word is by using a conjunction. The spies said, "Yes the land is flowing with milk and honey; nevertheless..." When they added the conjunction, "nevertheless," it did not matter what they would say after that. They were preparing to negate the word and promise of God. God had *said* He was giving them the land to possess.

Today we might say, "I know God's word says that He forgives all my sins and heals all my diseases, but..." It doesn't matter what you say after that. You are going to negate God's word and show you don't really believe what it says. You have a different opinion on the matter.

Or one might say, "Yes, I know God's word says that He will supply all my needs and that I should not worry; however...." Again, it doesn't matter what you say beyond that, you are about to say that you do not really believe in His promise, and your circumstances are greater than His word.

The eyes of faith show us how God sees things. If you want to know how God sees your situation, look at it through your eyes of faith. Look at it in light of what God's word says about it.

The righteous are not to fear a bad report. "He will not fear evil tidings; his heart is steadfast, trusting in the Lord" (Psalm 112:7).

Two Reports

Back to the spies. Ten of the twelve told how strongly

fortified the cities and how large the giants were, and they told of other obstacles and hindrances that stood in opposition to what God had promised. They reported on what they saw with their natural eyes.

As you read on through the account, you read of two men, Joshua and Caleb, who gave a completely different report of the same thing. The ten argued, "We are not able to go up against the people there, for they are too strong for us." Joshua and Caleb said, "We should by all means go up and take possession of it, for we surely will overcome it."

The ten saw only what they could see with their natural eyes. The two saw the same things, and *acknowledged* that they had seen the same things, but they also viewed the situation through the eyes of faith, their spiritual eyes. They saw things as God saw them.

The ten perceived the obstacles and hindrances as larger than God's promise. The two saw God's promise as larger than any obstacle or hindrance in the natural realm.

The crowd sided with the ten, entering into fear rather than faith. See Numbers 14:1-4. Joshua and Caleb tried once again to get the people to have faith in God's promise, but to no avail. See Numbers 14:6-10.

God's Response

God's response was that the ten who rejected His word would never go into the Promised Land. Only Joshua and Caleb, who saw the situation as God did, who saw through eyes of faith and agreed with God, would be able to go into the land of promise.

God said Caleb had "a different spirit" than the ten had. We see what that different spirit was: "But having the same spirit of faith, according to what is written, 'I believed, therefore I spoke,' we also believe, therefore we also speak" (2 Corinthians 4:13).

Why was it called the Promised Land? Because God promised it. When God gives a promise, the only question is who will receive it and walk in it and be a part of it.

God needed a people who could see and live by faith in Him, His word, and His promises. Faith is that which brings the promises of God's word into manifestation in our lives.

We must unite faith with His word, "For indeed we have had good news preached to us, just as they also; but the word they heard did not profit them, because it was not united by faith in those who heard" (Hebrews 4:2).

As we have seen, faith gives substance to our hopes and gives us a certainty of realities we do not yet see. Did you note the language of Joshua and Caleb as you read through the account? Words like *surely, certainly, we can do it because we have God's word on it.* Those are faith words. They believed the word of God and therefore spoke in accordance with His promise rather than the circumstances.

Faith persuades us, absolutely convinces us, that God will fulfill His word, that He is faithful to His word.

Obstacles or Opportunities

Natural eyes see natural things like giants, fortifications, strongholds, barriers, obstacles, hindrances, adversities, afflictions, storms, trials, troubles - natural things.

Spiritual eyes - the eyes of your heart - the eyes of faith see God's word and see it being fulfilled in spite of all the natural things that might shout out against it.

God wanted the people to see the obstacles and hindrances so they would know it was He who brought the victory. So they would give Him all glory and praise. So they would not say, "Look what we have done," but "Look what the *Lord* has done!"

It is the same in your life and mine. God wants us to see with our natural eyes all the things that seem to stand against us so we will call on Him, rely on Him, trust in Him, believe His word, and then give Him the honor and praise for the overcoming victory that is wrought.

Joshua and Caleb did not deny what the others reported seeing. They saw those things, too, with their natural eyes. They saw the giants, the obstacles, but their response was, "But God said..."

When thoughts come to you or circumstances surrounding you seem to oppose God's word, say, "But God says..."

God calls into being that which does not exist. See Romans 4:17. He doesn't deny what is, but calls forth something better and greater.

God saw the darkness, but called forth light. He didn't deny the darkness. He acknowledged it, but He saw something better!

Agreeing With God

Faith doesn't deny what our natural eyes see, but it calls forth what God says *can* be. Faith declares that the as yet unseen promise and word of God is as real as what our natural eyes can perceive.

Joshua and Caleb said, "If the Lord be pleased with us, nothing can stop us." See Numbers 14:8. What is it that pleases God?

"And without faith it is impossible to please Him, for he who comes to God must believe that He is and that He is a rewarder of those who seek Him" (Hebrews 11:6).

At this point you may be thinking, "I wish I had faith like Joshua and Caleb and Elisha." The good news is - you can.

You may have learned some musical notes, musical scores and terminology, but still can not play like a seasoned musician. You may be able to pass, dribble, and execute some plays, but still do not play basketball like a super star athlete. The difference is practice. With practice you get better at everything – including faith. More on that in a later chapter. Keep reading.

Chapter 3

❖ ❖ ❖

Faith Works

It is important to learn all you can about faith. To use the basketball analogy used earlier, you can learn to dribble, execute plays, run, pass, and maneuver; but if you never learn how to shoot a basket you will be of very limited use as a player. For that matter, *if any* of the components mentioned are missing you will be incomplete and ineffective as a basketball player.

It is the same with faith. There are various components; and if you are not aware of or proficient in them you might wrongly come to the conclusion that faith does not work. Faith does work. Real Bible faith works.

"For in Christ Jesus neither circumcision nor uncircumcision means anything, but faith working through love" (Galatians 5:6).

The Amplified Bible puts it this way: "...only faith activated and energized and expressed and working through love."

Faith activated, energized, expressed, and working! Faith works.

Quoting again from the Amplified Bible we read in 2nd Thessalonians 1:11, "With this in view we constantly pray for you, that our God may deem and count you worthy of (your) calling and (His) every gracious purpose of goodness, and with power complete in every particular, (your) work of faith, (faith which is that leaning of the whole human personality on God in absolute trust and confidence in His power, wisdom and goodness)."

The Word Works with Active Faith

Apostle Paul wrote to the church of Thessalonica, "...the word of God, which performs its work in you who believe" (1 Thessalonians 2:13).

We see in the above passages of Scripture that God's word works (is manifested) in those who believe it and whose faith is energized, activated, expressed, and working, bringing the unseen promises of God into the seen or natural realm.

Notice that this active and effective faith is related to the leaning of our whole personality on the Lord, relying on Him, and trusting in Him and the truth of His word.

Real faith does not work apart from an abiding relationship with the Lord. "I am the vine, you are the branches; he who abides in Me and I in him, he bears much fruit; for apart from Me you can do nothing" (John 15:5).

The reason some come to the conclusion that faith does not work is that they say they are operating in faith, but are not. I knew a man whose wife was diagnosed as terminally ill. I asked how we could join with him in prayer so we would be in agreement. In other words, I asked him where his faith was. What was he believing God would do?

His reply was that he knew God was going to heal her, so that is where he was putting his faith. She died, and I learned later that all the while he was saying he knew she would be healed, he was making funeral plans and arrangements for her death.

He was desperately hoping his wife would be healed, but let's look again at what Bible faith is.

"Now faith is the *assurance* of things hoped for, the *conviction* of things not seen" (Hebrews 11:1).

Faith and Hope are Not the Same

Faith is beyond hope. It is the *knowing* with assurance and conviction, beyond doubt, that what is hoped for will be manifested in accordance with God's word.

This illustration is in no way meant to be critical of the man. He was fearful and desperately hoping for his wife's healing, but it would be wrong to say he was in faith. So, it would be wrong to conclude that faith didn't work.

People come to the altar in church needing healing. They say they are standing on the word of God in faith for healing, but sometimes they really come out of fear. They dread the thought of having surgery or some other medical treatment, but they are not really convinced with absolute assurance that God is going to heal them.

There will be a later chapter on faith and healing, but we are noting here that one should not conclude that faith does not work because someone thought he was in faith but was not. He may have been hoping or even in fear or something else other than faith. Faith works.

Faith that works, that brings results, has three basic components: believing, speaking, and action.

We saw in an earlier chapter the "spirit of faith." We believe, therefore, we speak. Those are two components. James adds a third.

Works of Faith

"Even so faith, if it has no works, is dead, being by itself" (James 2:17). "For just as the body without the spirit is dead, so also faith without works is dead" (James 2:26).

Works of faith are actions or deeds that correspond to faith. Real faith includes believing the word of God with certainty, speaking forth what the word of God says (rather than focusing on your situation), and acting like what you say you believe and in accordance with what you speak.

What you believe, what you speak, and the actions you take are all in agreement. You are not acting one way but speaking another way, or believing something different from what you say you believe.

You Can't Fake Faith

Another area that some get into is trying to mimic someone else's faith. A person may hear great teaching on faith by someone who lives by faith and sees great results in his life because of it. But faith must become a revelation of truth for each individual.

Although it may be good to observe and learn from those who live an active faith life, each of us must develop his own faith by abiding in the Lord and allowing His word to abide in us.

There is a dramatic account of how attempting to imitate or mimic someone else's faith may turn out. We find it in the 19th chapter of the book of Acts.

"God was performing extraordinary miracles by the hand of Paul, so that handkerchiefs or aprons were even carried from his body to the sick, and the diseases left them and the evil spirits went out.

"But also some of the Jewish exorcists, who went from place to place, attempted to name over those who had the evil spirits the name of the Lord Jesus, saying, 'I adjure you by Jesus whom Paul preaches.'

"Seven sons of one Sceva, a Jewish chief priest, were doing this. And the evil spirit answered and said, 'I recognize

Jesus, and I know about Paul, but who are you?' And the man in whom was the evil spirit leaped on them and subdued all of them and overpowered them, so they fled out of that house naked and wounded" (Acts 19:11-16).

Jesus cast out demons, evil spirits. And because Paul had an abiding relationship with Jesus, he cast out demons, too. But the sons of Sceva and the Jewish priests had no relationship with Jesus. They used the same words Jesus and Paul used, but the results were quite different because they were only trying to mimic what they had seen others do.

If you want your faith to develop and work effectively, continue building an intimate relationship with Jesus. There will be more on strengthening your faith in a later chapter.

Chapter 4

❖ ❖ ❖

Faith Under Pressure

One of the most astounding Scriptures is found in James 1:2-4. Let's look at it from The Message Bible, a paraphrase that brings out some significant aspects of the passage.

"Consider it a sheer gift, friends, when tests and challenges come at you from all sides. You know that under pressure, your faith-life is forced into the open and shows its true colors. So don't try to get out of anything prematurely. Let it do its work so you become mature and well-developed, not deficient in any way."

Think of the various ways the word "colors" is used in our language. Three things come to mind:

1) A colored badge, ribbon or uniform that identifies the wearer or shows his connection with something or someone.

2) A flag or banner that shows what side a person is on.

3) Something that shows one's position or opinion.

A gang wears its colors to show its identity, which side it is on, and what its position is. The colors of a flag also reflect these three things.

In a sense, our faith gives us an identity. It shows our connection to something or someone. It is like a banner that shows which side or whose side we are on. It shows what our position or opinion is, whether we agree with God's word or not.

How Faith Responds to Trials

Now let's look at those verses from the NAS Bible, which is closer to the original language.

"Consider it all joy, my brethren, when you encounter various trials, knowing that the testing of your faith produces endurance. And let endurance have its perfect result, so that you may be perfect and complete, lacking in nothing."

The word "joy" here means "cheerfulness, calm delight, gladness, exceeding joy, peaceful joy." This verse is not for everyone. It is not for unbelievers, but for the brethren. The language here of "encountering" various trials implies being completely surrounded by them. It's not just about facing a single problem or storm of life. These verses speak of being completely immersed in trials and pressures.

Even when trials are enveloping you, when they are all around you, even then you can consider it all joy!

When trials or storms of life come, they force your faith

out into the open. They expose where your faith really lies. Is it on God and His word, or on the circumstances that surround you?

Job said, "When He has tried me, I shall come forth as gold" (Job 23:10).

Trials refine your faith and show you exactly where your faith is and how well you have developed it. Faith produces "endurance." In the original Greek language that word means "cheerful or hopeful endurance. Constancy, consistency, patience." Cheerful endurance filled with hope. It is not just gritting your teeth and bearing up under the pressure with a frown and a grumble. Consider it all joy!

How can one be joyful, calm, and at peace when things around him or her are falling apart? When things are not working out like he or she thought they would or should?

That is what we will find out as we go further into all of this.

Seeing Beyond the Trial

"Fixing our eyes on Jesus, the author and perfecter of faith, who for the joy set before Him endured the cross, despising the shame, and has sat down at the right hand of the throne of God" (Hebrews 12:2).

Notice that the words in this verse are similar to those in James 1:2-4: "Faith...joy...endured ...consider."

How could Jesus endure the pressure of the cross?

Because He looked beyond the trial to what was coming on the other side: the throne!

We, too, can learn to look beyond the difficult times to the victory that is on the other side. No storm lasts forever. Tornadoes, floods, hurricanes, and other natural storms may cause terrible damage, but none of them lasts forever. All will pass.

The same is true with our struggles in life. If we endure in faith, we will come out to the victory after the storm has passed and will be as James told us, "perfect, complete, and lacking in nothing." It is our faith that will bring us through and keep us connected to the Lord so we can draw upon His strength, power, and might.

Trials will tend to cause you to grow weary and lose heart. "Let us not lose heart in doing good, for in due time we will reap if we do not grow weary" (Galatians 6:9).

When trials come and you are under pressure, you may not want to contend further in the fight of faith. There will be a tendency to give in, to give up, but that is exactly the wrong thing to do. Giving up brings defeat, not victory. It will put you under, not over!

Consider it all joy, my brethren, when trials surround you. Your faith will give you strength. "The joy of the Lord is your strength" (Nehemiah 8:10).

Paul said he had learned to be content in all things. "I've learned to be content in whatever circumstances I am" (Philippians 4:11).

Transcending Faith

Paul had learned through experience and through his trust in the Lord that faith transcends the changing and often unpredictable circumstances in which we find ourselves.

He had learned there is something more eternal, more long-lasting than temporary circumstances. He learned that no matter what his circumstances, his faith would bring him through.

Consider some of the circumstances that surrounded him: "...in far more labors, in far more imprisonments, beaten times without number, often in danger of death. Five times I received from the Jews thirty-nine lashes. Three times I was beaten with rods, once I was stoned, three times I was shipwrecked, a night and a day I have spent in the deep. I have been on frequent journeys, in dangers from rivers, dangers from robbers, dangers from my countrymen, dangers from the Gentiles, dangers in the city, dangers in the wilderness, dangers on the sea, and dangers among false brethren. I have been in labor and hardship, through many sleepless nights, in hunger and thirst, often without food, in cold and exposure. Apart from such external things, there is the daily pressure on me of concern for all the churches" (2 Corinthians 11:23-28).

What did all these things have in common? They all passed. Paul's unwavering faith brought him through them all. He endured, he stayed consistent, and he did not give in. He did not give up.

In all these things he was hurt, disappointed and betrayed...but he learned there was something lasting that would remain when all his trials were over.

Significance and Security in Christ

"Weeping may last for the night, but a shout of joy comes in the morning" (Psalm 30:5).

"In Thy presence is fullness of joy" (Psalm 16:11).

Despite all that Paul went through, he was still able to stand before the king and say, "So, King Agrippa, I did not prove disobedient to the heavenly vision..." (Acts 26:19).

Paul had found his significance and security in Christ and was able to fulfill the calling God had placed on his life. He was able to fulfill his destiny in the Lord.

He stood before the king with scars and bruises, with a heart that had been broken, with disappointments still within his memory; but he could still declare he had been faithful to what God had asked him to do.

Jesus endured the cross for the glory on the other side so He could say to the Father through tears and heartache, having been misunderstood, betrayed, turned against, scoffed, mocked, His faith tested, "Father, I was not disobedient to the heavenly vision."

You and I can endure in faith and one day stand before the King of all kings, and although beaten, betrayed, disappointed, and still remembering times our hearts were broken, we can say, "O King, I was not disobedient to the heavenly vision."

We *can* say that, if we endure in faith to the end!

Faith Shows Which Side You are On

Paul's faith was forced out into the open and seen by all. There was no question regarding to whom he was connected, which side he was on, or what his position or opinion was. There was no question regarding with whom he agreed.

Asaph lamented over what seemed to be the unfairness of life. "But as for me, my feet came close to stumbling, my steps had almost slipped. For I was envious of the arrogant as I saw the prosperity of the wicked. For there are no pains in their death, and their body is fat. They are not in trouble as other men, nor are they plagued like mankind" (Psalm 73:2-5).

Then he came into the presence of the Lord and received a whole new perspective. See verses 16-17. He finally concluded, "But as for me, the nearness of God is my good. I have made the Lord God my refuge, that I may tell of all Your works" (Psalm 73:28).

Asaph discovered, actually learned, something that transcends the unfairness of life and difficult circumstances. The nearness of God was his good.

Let us look back at Paul once again and see what he learned about enduring in faith and how it affected the way he lived.

Paul was being transported as a prisoner by ship when a terrible storm arose. The ship and its crew were surrounded by the raging storm.

But Paul had a word from God and he put his faith on that word, not on the storm that was enveloping them. An angel stood beside him and said, "Do not be afraid, Paul. You must stand before Caesar; and behold, God has granted you all those who are sailing with you" (Acts 27:24).

After losing all their cargo and having the ship torn apart on the rocks, the crew and passengers all made it safely ashore to an island. There, while gathering wood for a fire, Paul was bitten by a poisonous snake.

"However he shook the creature off into the fire and suffered no harm" (Acts 28:5). When we have a word from God to put our faith on, we just need to shake things off as they attack us, knowing that God's word will be manifested if we stay in enduring faith.

Now read on through the rest of Acts 28 and see what Paul did. He could have sat around the fire asking God, "Why me?" Or he could have prayed that God would deliver him out of his trial.

Instead he discovered there were sick people on the island who needed to be healed. In his own time of trial, Paul healed all the people on the island. Like Paul, as you learn to live a life of faith, *you* can be a blessing to others even while you are in a trial yourself!

Result of Enduring Faith

Remember, James said if we count it all joy and endure in faith we will come through perfect, complete, and lacking in nothing.

"After this had happened, the rest of the people on the island who had diseases were coming to him and getting cured. They also honored us with many marks of respect; and when we were setting sail, they supplied us with all we needed" (Acts 28:9-10). They were supplied with all they needed! They were lacking nothing!

God had told Paul that he would stand before Caesar. Paul then knew with assurance that neither shipwreck nor snake bite would prevent the word of God from being fulfilled.

Paul had learned that no matter how long it took, no matter what he had to go through to get there, his focus was to be obedient to God's word and to do the work he was called to do. And God's word would be fulfilled in and through him.

If you will learn not to get sidetracked with shipwrecks and storms and trials and various kinds of pressure, you will have the assurance of the victory on the other side!

If you will endure with consistency, knowing God will use you to bless others even in the trial, then you will experience the calm, peaceful joy of the Lord that will give you strength to carry on. And you can do so rejoicing!

Know that when the pressures of life come and your

faith is forced out into the open, you will declare who you are connected with and what your opinion of the matter is. All will know whose side you are on!

We will take a more detailed look later in this book at how our faith is tested.

Chapter 5

❖ ❖ ❖

Faith And The Storms Of Life

"Therefore everyone who hears these words of Mine and acts on them may be compared to a wise man who built his house on the rock. And the rain fell, and the floods came, and the winds blew and slammed against that house and yet it did not fall, for it had been founded on the rock.

"Everyone who hears these words of Mine and does not act on them will be like a foolish man who built his house on the sand. The rain fell, and the floods came, and the winds blew and slammed against that house and it fell - - and great was its fall" (Matthew 7:24-27).

Jesus was speaking of two responses to His words: doing what He said to do or not doing what He said to do. Each choice had a consequence.

This passage of Scripture, of course, can apply to anything that Jesus said to do. Thus it can apply to faith. What did He say about faith?

"Have faith in God. Truly I say to you, whoever says to this mountain, 'Be taken up and cast into the sea,' and does not doubt in his heart, but believes that what he says is going to happen, it will be granted him. Therefore I say to you, all things for which you pray and ask, believe that you received them, and they will be granted you" (Mark 11:22-24).

If we build our house (life) on the rock (the word of God) and have faith in Him and abide in Him, the storms of life will not destroy us.

Faith Brings Victory

Living by faith does not mean there will not be storms. Storms come against the righteous and the unrighteous, but faith in God will bring us through the storms to victory.

Peter put it this way: "In this you greatly rejoice, even though now for a little while, if necessary, you have been distressed by various trials, so that the proof of your faith, being more precious than gold which is perishable, even though tested by fire, may be found to result in praise and glory and honor at the revelation of Jesus Christ..." (1 Peter 1:6-7).

Doesn't that sound a lot like what James recorded, as we read in the previous chapter? When our faith is tested or forced out into the open, we can rejoice because the result will be "praise and glory and honor as Jesus Christ is revealed" through it all.

In the last chapter, we followed Paul through shipwreck

and snake bite and saw how his consistent faith brought him from the beginning to the end so that, when it was over, he had lost nothing. And while going through the trials, he healed all the people on the island where he took temporary refuge.

Faith in the Dungeon

We might also remember what Paul did while in the inner dungeon of the jail. He was not feeling sorry for himself or throwing a pity party. He was not praying for deliverance out of the jail. He was looking for an opportunity to do the work of the Lord even in the midst of his trial, which he knew one way or another would pass, as all trials do, while he remained in faith.

"The crowd rose up together against them, and the chief magistrates tore their robes off them and proceeded to order them to be beaten with rods. When they had struck them with many blows, they threw them into prison, commanding the jailer to guard them securely; and he, having received such a command, threw them into the inner prison and fastened their feet in the stocks.

"But about midnight Paul and Silas were praying and singing hymns of praise to God, and the prisoners were listening to them; and suddenly there came a great earthquake, so that the foundations of the prison house were shaken; and immediately all the doors were opened and everyone's chains were unfastened.

"When the jailer awoke and saw the prison doors

opened, he drew his sword and was about to kill himself, supposing that the prisoners had escaped.

"But Paul cried out with a loud voice, saying, 'Do not harm yourself, for we are all here!' And he called for lights and rushed in, and trembling with fear he fell down before Paul and Silas, and after he brought them out, he said, 'Sirs, what must I do to be saved?'

"They said, 'Believe in the Lord Jesus and you will be saved, you and your household.' And they spoke the word of the Lord to him together with all who were in his house. And he took them that very hour of the night and washed their wounds, and immediately he was baptized, he and his entire household. And he brought them into his house and set food before them, and rejoiced greatly, having believed in God with his whole household" (Acts 16:22-34).

Great rejoicing resulted as Jesus Christ was revealed, just as Peter had said.

Bless the Lord at All Times

Paul and Silas were doing what the Psalmist did: "I will bless the Lord at all times. His praise shall continually be in my mouth" (Psalm 34:1).

Paul was consistent, constant, in his faith. He walked in faith before being jailed, while in jail, and after he was released from jail. He blessed the Lord at all times and continually had the praises of God in his mouth, because he had learned that faith always works.

Habakkuk, too, had learned that faith in God would bring him through any situation. "Though the fig tree should not blossom and there be no fruit on the vines, though the yield of the olive should fail and the fields produce no food, though the flock should be cut off from the fold and there be no cattle in the stalls, yet I will exult in the Lord, I will rejoice in the God of my salvation. The Lord God is my strength, and He has made my feet like hinds' feet, and makes me walk on my high places" (Habakkuk 3:17-19).

When we live by faith we can rejoice in all circumstances, because we know that God will bring us through as we trust in Him and rely on Him.

All kinds of storms have raged against God's people. Our response to the storm reveals where our faith is and how much we trust in and have confidence in the Lord.

Let's encourage ourselves by looking at some other examples of faith which show its true colors and how God responded to the faith that was expressed.

Jehoshaphat, when faced with a multitude of the enemy forces, cried out to God in front of all the people and declared, "O Lord, the God of our fathers, are You not God in the heavens? And are You not ruler over all the kingdoms of the nations? Power and might are in Your hand so that no one can stand against You" (2 Chronicles 20:6).

As you read the whole account here, you see that Jehoshaphat was clearly putting his faith in God in the time of his great need.

God's Response

God's response to his faith was spoken prophetically through Jahaziel, and he said, "Listen, all Judah and the inhabitants of Jerusalem and King Jehoshaphat: thus says the Lord to you, 'Do not fear or be dismayed because of this great multitude, for the battle is not yours, but God's'" (2 Chronicles 20:15).

So the people went out and began to sing praises to God, and the Lord confused their enemies to the point that they began to fight against one another. "When they began singing and praising, the Lord set ambushes against the sons of Ammon, Moab and Mount Seir, who had come against Judah; so they were routed" (2 Chronicles 20:22).

Believing God's Word

There was a time that Jericho was a well fortified and closed city. God spoke to Joshua and said, "See, I have given Jericho into your hand, with its king and the valiant warriors" (Joshua 6:1-2).

God told Joshua to see that He had given Jericho to him, when the city was still closed and well fortified. God wanted Joshua to look at the situation through the eyes of faith and put his faith on the word that God had given him. Are you beginning to see how this all works?

You know the story. God gave Joshua specific instructions regarding walking around the city seven times and then shouting. Joshua followed His instructions and the walls fell down.

It wasn't the marching or shouting that brought down the walls. It was Joshua's obedience to God's word and putting faith on His word. Remember the three elements of faith? Joshua *believed* God's word, *spoke* God's word, and *acted* upon the word in a corresponding way.

If Joshua wasn't fully assured that the word of God would be manifested as it had been spoken to him, it is unlikely he would have marched and shouted.

"Faith is the assurance of things hoped for, the conviction of things not yet seen" (Hebrews 11:1).

In the 7th chapter of Judges, we read an account of Gideon and his army. Gideon started out with 32,000 men in his army as he received instructions from God, who told him they were to go out and defeat the Midianites.

It would have taken some kind of faith to take 32,000 warriors into battle, because it has been estimated that the enemy forces may have been around 135,000. But God wanted Gideon to go in real, strong faith. So as you read the account, you see the various ways in which Gideon was instructed to reduce his army to a mere 300 men. Why would God have done that?

"The Lord said to Gideon, 'The people who are with you are too many for Me to give Midian into their hands, for Israel would become boastful, saying, 'My own power has delivered me'" (Judges 7:2).

It took real faith for Gideon to go up against such a large number of warriors with only 300 men, but he believed God when He promised him the victory. In other words, he put his faith upon the word of God, which is where our faith needs to be.

A Woman of Faith

In the 4th chapter of 2 Kings, we read the account of a woman of great faith. Her husband had died and her creditor had come to take two of her children away to be his slaves.

The prophet Elisha came along and found that her food was gone and all she had left was a jar of oil. He instructed her to go around the neighborhood and collect all the vessels she could and bring them home.

When she did, he told her to go inside her home and pour the little bit of oil she had left from her jar into the many vessels. Would that not have taken a lot of faith?

She did as she was told by the prophet, and the oil continued to be multiplied and pour out until the very last container was filled. "When the vessels were full, she said to her son, 'Bring me another vessel.' And he said to her, 'There is not one vessel more.' And the oil stopped" (2 Kings 4:6).

"Then she came and told the man of God. And he said, 'Go, sell the oil and pay your debt, and you and your sons can live on the rest'" (2 Kings 4:7).

The woman was in the midst of a storm of life when it looked like all was lost, but her faith in God's word spoken through the prophet brought forth enough oil to pay off all her bills and set up an income for both her and her sons. Is that not what James spoke of when he said if we would endure in faith, we would come through "perfect, complete, and lacking in nothing?" Faith works, even in the storms of life.

Chapter 6

❖ ❖ ❖

Ever-Enlarging Faith

Sequoia trees live a long time and become quite large because they don't stop growing. Our muscles become strong when we keep exercising them. On the other hand, when a plant stops growing, it begins to die; and when muscles are not used, they begin to atrophy.

In the same way, faith must also continue to grow and be exercised in order to become stronger and more effective, as opposed to being weak and ineffective.

"We ought always to give thanks to God for you, brethren, as is only fitting, because your faith is greatly enlarged, and the love of each one of you toward one another grows ever greater" (2 Thessalonians 1:3).

Paul recognized that both faith and love were increasing in the believers at Thessalonica. "Your faith is greatly enlarged." Other versions have translated this as follows: "Your faith is growing more and more," "Your faith groweth exceedingly," and "Your faith keeps growing all the time."

Developing your Faith

We receive a measure of faith when we are born again. See Romans 12. Then we spend a lifetime developing it, enlarging it, and strengthening it.

You can build your muscles up and become strong, but if you quit exercising, then no matter how strong you were, your muscles will atrophy. After awhile, you will be as weak as you would have been had you never exercised. It is the same with your faith.

Remember that we read from the Amplified Bible earlier that, "...faith activated and energized and express and working..." (Galatians 5:6). This speaks of constantly, consistently, active faith.

Faith always connects with the word of God. It unites with the word, and co-mingles with it. The result is like two liquids that come together to become one and cannot then be separated. Review Hebrews 4:2.

The word of God awakens, or stirs up, our faith. It gives hope, then gives us an assurance beyond hope that the word of God is real and true, and will be manifested in our life.

"For with God nothing is ever impossible, and no word from God shall be without power or impossible of fulfillment" (Luke 1:37, Amplified Bible).

In Proverbs, Chapter 30, we see that God's word is true. It is tested. The Psalmist declares, "The word of God is forever settled in Heaven" (Psalm 119:89).

Jesus instructed that we pray, "Thy will be done on earth as it is in Heaven." The truth and reliability of God's word is settled in Heaven. Now, we need to settle it in our hearts.

Faith does not debate God's word. Faith says, "If God says it, I believe it. I receive it by faith. It is settled. No debate."

"The grass withers, the flower fades, but the word of our God stands forever" (Isaiah 40:8).

"Let us hold fast the confession of our hope without wavering, for He who promised is faithful" (Hebrews 10:23).

"...the word of God, which also performs its work in you who believe" (1 Thessalonians 2:13b).

Ever-Enlarging Faith

We are to live a life of faith. That is God's will for our lives. Whatever is not of faith is sin. See Romans 14:23. If we are not living by faith, we are missing the mark. We are missing God's will. We are in sin.

We are to develop our faith. It is to be ever-enlarging and increasingly effective.

It took faith for David to face and slay Goliath. But that was not the first time David used his faith. He had confidence and was full of faith when facing the giant because he was able to recall how he had already slain a bear and a lion. He knew that his unrelenting faith in God would bring victory in this case also.

The giant loomed as a mountain before him; but David had overcoming, mountain-moving faith. The giant was huge; the hindrance that stood before him was huge. But David knew his God was bigger!

David had operated in faith before, and he knew that experience would serve him well in his current time of need. We exercise our faith just like we exercise our muscles and our mind: by using them constantly and consistently.

Noah had a word from God: Build an ark. Noah put his faith on that word, put action to it that corresponded, and built the ark. He kept his eyes on the Lord, not on the dry ground or the cloudless sky or the scoffers and mockers; nor on the clock or the calendar.

He built the ark; and God's word was manifested in his life as he and his family boarded the ark and were saved from disaster. It all happened just as God said it would. The promise became a reality.

Noah endured, acting on God's word for over a hundred years. "…that you may not be sluggish, but imitators of those who through faith and patience inherit the promises" (Hebrews 6:12). A chapter on faith and patience will come later.

Walking by Faith, Not by Sight

As you seek to follow the Lord and pursue His plans and purposes for your life, you will encounter times when nothing around you seems to agree with what God has said.

At these times, you must act on His word alone.

Moses had only the word of God when Pharaoh's army was pressing in and an open sea faced him and God's people. All he had was the word of God that God would deliver them.

Standing on that word alone, he raised his staff as instructed. The result was one of the greatest miracles ever recorded. The sea parted, and God fulfilled His promise in response to Moses' faith. His word was manifested in their lives. "For we walk by faith, not by sight" (2 Corinthians 5:7).

"Therefore, do not throw away your confidence, which has a great reward. For you have need of endurance, so that when you have done the will of God, you may receive what was promised" (Hebrews 10:35-36).

Another one who was not willing to throw away her confidence in the Lord, even when she saw no evidence of the word manifested, was the woman we read about in the 9th chapter of Matthew.

"And behold, a woman who had been suffering from a hemorrhage for twelve years came up behind Him and touched the fringe of His cloak; for she was saying to herself, 'If I only touch His garment, I shall get well'" (Matthew 9:20-21).

She believed she would be healed; she spoke it. Then she acted in accordance to what she believed and spoke. She was not merely hoping it might happen. She said, "I *shall* get well."

When she touched His garment, Jesus said to her, "'Daughter, take courage; your faith has made you well.' And at once the woman was made well."

This was not a mind over matter thing. It was not that she got psyched up somehow. It was not some "New Age visualization." It was the power of God and His promise of healing that was released, because she exercised her faith and confidence in Him.

"Bless the Lord, O my soul; and all that is within me, bless His holy name. Bless the Lord, O my soul, and forget none of His benefits; He pardons all your iniquities; He heals all your diseases" (Psalm 103:1-3).

A chapter on faith and healing is forthcoming; but see here how energizing and activating and expressing her faith brought the promise of God into manifestation in her life. And, don't you know her faith became even stronger when she experienced His promised healing power!

Activating Your Faith

Develop your faith. Use and exercise it. It will become an absolute, unwavering trust, confidence, and belief in God's word. It will become a way of life with great rewards.

Keep your eyes fixed upon Jesus who, according to Hebrews 12:2, is "the author and perfecter of faith." He gave you a measure of faith and He will help you develop it.

A blind man named Bartimaeus heard that Jesus was

coming down the road. Faith was awakened. Faith was stirred up within him. He cried out, "Jesus, son of David, have mercy on me!" (Mark 10:47).

People told him to be quiet and quit making a scene. But Bartimaeus persisted and cried out all the louder. Jesus heard his cry and called him forth. When Bartimaeus came to Jesus, He said, "Go, your faith has made you well" (Mark 10:52).

Bartimaeus was healed of his blindness. Jesus said it was because he put action to his faith, and his faith brought forth the promise of healing.

As you develop your faith, there will be times when you have to be intentional, even aggressive. Others may try to shut you down, but you have a word from the Lord and you want to see it manifested in your life. Bartimaeus desired to bring forth the promise of God's word more than he desired to please those around him by being quiet and shutting down his faith.

If you want to develop overcoming, mountain-moving faith, you will need to desire it more than you desire to please those around you who do not understand faith. Developing your faith must be a priority in your life.

There are things that will rise up against you to hinder your ever-enlarging faith. We will look at some of those in a later chapter.

Continue on in faith, established and steadfast and not moved away from the hope of the gospel that you have heard. See Colossians 1:23.

How we respond forces our faith out into the open, to show its true colors. So what was Job's response? "When He has tried me, I shall come forth as gold" (Job 23:10).

Refining Faith

When we see the words "tried" or "tested" in the Scriptures, they usually mean the same thing. They are actually refiner's or smelter's terms. Extracting gold from the rock that contains it requires both heat and pressure.

When I first visited a gold mine and observed the process of mining and refining the gold, I was impressed with the huge piles of rock from which came gold only the size of a pea. Yet, that small piece of gold had value that far exceeded what it was worth while it was still a part of the rock. It was interesting to watch as tons of rock were exposed to heat and pressure to yield a result so minuscule.

Job received a lot of heat and pressure from his circumstances, from his friends, and from all that was going on around him. Yet he apparently had a revelation telling him that if he continued to trust the Lord through it all, he would come out as gold; that he would have far greater value than he had before.

His faith brought him through the most horrible of situations because it made him continue to trust in God as he endured.

Remember that James wrote about what would happen if we endured in faith even while he was enveloped in various trials. "Consider it all joy, my brethren, when you encounter various trials, knowing that the testing of your faith produces endurance. And let endurance have its perfect result, so that you may be perfect and complete, lacking in nothing" (James 1:2-4).

How did Job come out after enduring in faith? "The Lord restored the fortunes of Job when he prayed for his friends, and the Lord increased all that Job had twofold" (Job 42:10). He came through all the trials perfect and complete, not only lacking for nothing, but with twice the amount he had lost! He came forth from it all as gold.

Another Test

Let's look at a less dramatic, yet equally significant, example of faith being tested. "Therefore Jesus, lifting up His eyes and seeing that a large crowd was coming to Him, said to Philip, 'Where are we to buy bread, so that these may eat?' This He was saying to test him, for He Himself knew what He was intending to do" (John 6:5-6).

Jesus had been healing and casting demons out of multitudes of people and setting them free. Thousands of people had gathered as the sick were being brought to Him for healing.

Philip's reply was that even if they had 200 days worth of wages with which to buy food, it wouldn't be enough for even a tiny bit for each person. Philip was basically saying this is an impossible situation!

Jesus told Philip to have the people sit down. About 5,000 men were there; we don't know how many women and children might have been there also. He then took five loaves of bread and two very small fish from a boy in the crowd. He lifted them to Heaven and gave thanks for what they had. The food was then distributed to the thousands of people, and after they all had their fill, there were 12 baskets of leftovers.

Surely, as Philip saw what his own response was to the test of his faith and Jesus' response, he must have realized that he needed to develop his faith.

As Jesus gave thanks for what they had, He was exercising or expressing His faith that God would use it to provide for their need. He was assured that everything would work out as He relied on the Father to provide.

The result of the faith He expressed? Perfect and complete, lacking in nothing. Not only was there no lack, there was provision left over.

How do *you* respond when *your* faith is being tested? When heat and pressure is applied to your life and your circumstances? Where is your focus and attention given, to the problem or the solution?

Faith sees things as God sees them. He sees the end from the beginning. He looked beyond the darkness to the light. He looked beyond the cross to the throne.

Abraham's Faith

Let's take another look at faith being tried. "Now it

came about after these things, that God tested Abraham, and said to him 'Abraham!' And he said, 'Here I am'" (Genesis 22:1).

Reading on through the 22nd chapter of Genesis, we see a remarkable account of a man's faith being tested. Would Abraham follow through on the word of God? Would he rely on God, or would he be moved by what he saw in the natural?

God instructed him to take his only son whom he loved up on the mountain and sacrifice him on the altar.

"Then they came to the place of which God had told him; and Abraham built the altar there and arranged the wood, and bound his son Isaac and laid him on the altar, on top of the wood. Abraham stretched out his hand and took the knife to slay his son" (Genesis 22:9-10).

Abraham's faith was being tested. His obedience was being tried. Abraham was showing the true colors of his faith.

Then, "the angel of the Lord called to him from heaven and said, 'Abraham, Abraham!' And he said, 'Here I am.' He said, 'Do not stretch out your hand against the lad, and do nothing to him; for now I know that you fear God, since you have not withheld your son, your only son, from Me'" (Genesis 22:11-12).

The Purpose of Tests

What is the purpose of having our faith tested? What is

the purpose of any test? It is to see how we are progressing, to see where we stand.

Students generally do not look forward to tests in school. They view them as a negative experience. That is because they have not been taught the true purpose of tests and have not been shown the positive side.

One reason students fear tests is that they do not know what the teacher is going to ask on the test.

When I taught high school biology students before I entered into the ministry, I would give them, in writing, several objectives for each day's lesson. The students were told they would learn many things, but they could be assured that when it came time for a test, the questions would be based on those objectives.

That took out a lot of the guess work. The students knew that if they mastered the daily objectives, they would do well on the test. They did not have to wonder what I would ask or not ask on the test.

After the test, we would always review the correct answers. The students were told that the important thing is to learn the material. If they learned it before the test, that would be best. But if there were something they missed, they could learn it from the review and at least they would learn it.

God has given us objectives in His word. When He tests us, it will be so that we can see how we are progressing in our faith; so we will know how well we are doing at believing in, trusting in, and expressing His word.

God will give us many opportunities to learn His ways and to learn how to live by faith, and tests will show us how we are doing. There are times when our faith is tested and we pass with relative ease. We see that our faith is working and working well, just as God said that it would. That encourages us.

However, there are other times when we may not do so well and realize our faith is weak. We will know that we are not really relying on the Lord, not really expressing our trust in Him. But, we will learn something from it all; we are strengthened in our faith, and will do better next time.

"The word of the Lord tested him" (Psalm 105:19).

"I will refine them as silver is refined, and test them as gold is tested" (Zechariah 13:9).

Don't Avoid Tests

Do not avoid the tests of your faith. Remember that the test is refining your faith, burning away the dross, and removing that which is not real and pure faith.

As your faith is tested, you can rejoice when you see that it is effective in bringing forth the blessings and promises of God. And you can be encouraged even when it does not seem to be working, knowing that as you endure and continue to abide in the Lord and His word continues to abide in you, that you will eventually come forth as gold!

Chapter 8

❖ ❖ ❖

Faith And Patience

"Every good thing given and every perfect gift is from above, coming down from the Father of lights, with whom there is no variation or shifting shadow" (James 1:17).

Our unchanging Heavenly Father has a storehouse in Heaven filled with His blessings and promises, all gifts that are good and perfect. He longs to give gifts to those who will receive them by faith.

"Blessed be the God and Father of our Lord Jesus Christ, who has blessed us with every spiritual blessing in the heavenly places in Christ" (Ephesians 1:3). Again, we see that our Heavenly Father has blessings stored up for us.

"For as many as are the promises of God, in Him they are yes; therefore also through Him is our Amen to the glory of God through us" (2 Corinthians 1:20).

All of God's promises are "yes" in Him. When we go to God and say, "Lord, I see in Your word that You have forgiven all my sins and have healed all my diseases. Is that right? Is that meant for me?" His response is, "Yes."

We declare that He is our comforter in times of trouble and we say, "Can that be a promise that I can receive by trusting in You?" His response is, "Yes." For as many as His promises are, his responses are all "Yes."

And also through Him is our "Amen," all to the glory of God. When we say, "Amen," that literally means, "Let it be done as You have said."

When He shows us His promises and affirms they are all "Yes," then we express our faith and say, "Amen, I agree with You. If You said it, I believe it, I trust in it, and I'll rely on it, because You said it is so!"

"For this reason we also constantly thank God that when you received the word of God which you heard from us, you accepted it not as the word of men, but for what it really is, the word of God, which also performs its work in you who believe" (1 Thessalonians 1:13).

You Must Believe

His word performs its work in those who believe! When we say, "Amen" to His word, it is manifested. It performs its work in us.

We need to realize that faith must get hold of God's word. We need a Scriptural basis for our faith. We need a word from God for our faith. God may speak something into your spirit, but it will always agree with His written word, the Bible.

We should also know that Heaven does not change. God does not change. His word does not change.

Any breakdown in our receiving God's blessings, His promises, His provision occurs in *our* faith and/or *our* patience.

"...that you will not be sluggish, but imitators of those who through faith and patience inherit the promises" (Hebrews 6:12).

Patience

It is by faith and patience that the promises are inherited, are received. That bothers some people because of their concept of what patience is. To many, exercising patience is taking a deep breath, gritting their teeth and, with a grumble, wondering why something cannot happen *now*!

Let us take a look at what patience really is. In the English language it is defined as follows:

a) the will or ability to wait or endure without complaint;

b) steadfastness, endurance, perseverance in performing a task.

In the Greek language of the New Testament patience is defined as the following:

a) patient endurance;

b) cheerful or hopeful endurance, constancy, patient waiting.

Patience includes enduring or waiting, without complaint! It is staying in faith cheerfully! It is persevering with rejoicing until the promise comes into the reality of our life!

One dictionary definition of "endurance" is "to persevere under hardship without flinching." Apostle Paul wrote to the believers at Thessalonica, "Therefore, we ourselves speak proudly of you among the churches of God for your perseverance and faith in the midst of all your persecutions and afflictions which you endure" (2 Thessalonians 1:4).

He was praising the people who remained in faith, persevered, and endured even while surrounded by persecutions and afflictions. They weren't just lying down and playing dead; rather they were pressing on with faith and patience, actively exercising both! Their victory had not yet come, but they were not knocked off course just because their circumstances did not line up with the promises and blessings of God.

Hold On

The writer of the book of Hebrews gives great advice: "Therefore, do not throw away your confidence, which has a great reward. For you have need of endurance, so that when you have done the will of God, you may receive what was promised" (Hebrews 10:35-36).

Faith involves confidence in God and in His word. Faith assures us of the great rewards that can be obtained if we do not throw our confidence away.

Remember, "faith is the assurance of things hoped for, the conviction of things not yet seen."

When you wait in faith and patience, "...you will receive what was promised."

"...knowing that the testing of your faith produces endurance. And let endurance have its perfect result, so that you may be perfect and complete, lacking in nothing" (James 1:3-4). Endurance is patience. Endurance is perseverance. Endurance is staying power, continuing to believe in and trust in the Lord.

Faith and patience result in great rewards. You come through perfect, complete and lacking in nothing.

Waiting for the Manifestation

Jesus said, "Wait for what the Father has promised, 'which,' He said, 'you heard of from Me; for John baptized with water, but you will be baptized with the Holy Spirit not many days from now'" (Acts 1:4-5).

Jesus said the Father had made a promise. They were to receive the mighty baptism in the Holy Spirit. But it was not to be received at that moment. They were to go and wait for the promise to be manifested.

We might wonder what would have happened if they had all gone their own way, grumbling and complaining that the promise did not come at that moment.

But they did not do that. Instead, they gathered together in faith, with one mind and one accord, in the upper room. And the promise came, in the fullness of time. Read about it in Acts, Chapter 2, and in the rest of the book of Acts.

Part of the fruit of the reborn human spirit is patience. See Galatians 5:22.

Waiting. How many times do we throw away our assurance, our confidence, just before the answer comes? How many times do we miss a miracle by a minute?

Missing a Miracle by a Minute

- **Mary:** One minute a virgin, the next pregnant with the Son of God.

- **Jonah:** One minute in the belly of a fish, the next minute on dry land.

- **Abraham & Sarah:** One minute a barren womb, the next pregnant, the beginning of the promise of God, Father of many nations.

- **Lazarus:** One minute dead in a tomb, the next responding to the call of God and resurrected to new life.

- **Widow:** One moment had nothing but a little oil, some moments later her house was full.

- **Jailer:** One minute lost, the next minute saved by the

Holy Spirit working through Paul the prisoner.

What if Bartimaeus had kept quiet like they told him to? One minute he would have been blind, and the next minute the same, possibly for the rest of his life. But he reached for the promise, the provision of God; so he was blind one minute, and he could see the next.

What if the man with the withered hand had not responded to the word of God? But he did. He had a withered hand one minute, but was normal the next minute.

How many miracles might you have participated in had you waited a little longer?

One minute the lame man could not walk. Then Jesus told him to pick up his bed and walk. What if he had not obeyed? But he did. He was lame one minute, and then he was walking the next minute.

Cheerful Patience

How many miracles have you missed because you gave in too soon? Maybe another day, maybe another week or month, or maybe another minute and it would have been manifested.

We put our faith on the word of God and then wait with cheerful patience, knowing the promise is ours. We do whatever action is in concert with our faith to keep it alive. Otherwise our faith is dead. Faith without works is dead.

Remain cheerful while waiting for the manifestation

of the promise. Continue to agree with what God has said. Serve others while waiting! The reward is great; the result is perfect.

Continue abiding in Him. "If you abide in Me and My words abide in you, ask whatever you wish, and it shall be done for you" (John 15:7).

Receive by faith His precious and magnificent promises. Hold on to them by abiding patience, active patience. Not lethargy, but active and alive patience. The end result is that we are able to partake of His divine nature.

"...His divine power has granted to us everything pertaining to life and godliness, through the true knowledge of Him who called us by His own glory and excellence. For by these He has granted to us His precious and magnificent promises, so that by them you may become partakers of the divine nature, having escaped the corruption that is in the world by lust" (2 Peter 1:3-4).

We are not putting God out when we receive His provisions by faith. We are not bothering Him when we receive His promises. It pleases Him and brings Him honor and glory.

We need to develop and strengthen our faith. We need to activate and cultivate our faith. We need to energize and awaken our faith and our patience.

The result? Overcoming, mountain-moving faith!

Chapter 9

❖ ❖ ❖

Hindrances To Faith

"Be of sober spirit, be on the alert. Your adversary, the devil, prowls around like a roaring lion, seeking someone to devour. But resist him, firm in your faith..." (2 Peter 5:8-9a).

Your adversary, your opponent, your enemy will attempt to distract you, even to devour you. You resist him by remaining firm in your faith.

In this chapter we will explore some of the many ways he will endeavor to get you out of faith, because he knows he cannot defeat a Christ-follower who is living in strong faith.

Worry

Worry is sin. "...and whatever is not from faith is sin" (Romans 14:23b). Worry has never obtained one promise of God for you. Worry has not done one positive thing for you. *It cannot*, because worry is sin.

"Be anxious for nothing, but in everything by prayer and supplication with thanksgiving let your requests be made known to God" (Philippians 4:6). In other words, be anxious for nothing. Do not worry about anything. Fret not. Trust in and rely on God to help you through any and all circumstances of life as you stay in faith.

Fear

When surrounded by troubling circumstances, the disciples were fearful. They were in a boat, and a great storm came upon them. Jesus was asleep in the back of the boat. They cried out to Him to save them. Read the account in Matthew 8:23-26.

When awakened, Jesus rebuked the storm and all became calm. He asked the disciples, "Why are you afraid, you men of little faith?"

Faith and fear are opponents. Each brings different results. God wants you in faith so His power can work in and through you. Your adversary wants you in fear so *his* power can work in and through you.

"For God has not given us a spirit of timidity (fear), but of power and love and discipline" (2 Timothy 1:7). We are to live by faith, not fear. Fear will hinder your faith. Faith will overcome your fear.

Doubt

"But he must ask in faith without any doubting, for

the one who doubts is like the surf of the sea, driven and tossed by the wind. For that man ought not expect that he will receive anything from the Lord, being a double-minded man, unstable in all his ways" (James 1:6-7).

Doubt produces instability in one's life. Faith produces confidence and stability. Settle the word of God in your heart, and you need not worry, fear or doubt.

Unbelief

Jesus spoke to some people at Cana of Galilee, where he had performed a miracle. They evidently wanted to see more miracles and enjoy the benefits of them, but were not putting their faith in God's word. He said to them, "Unless you people see signs and wonders, you simply will not believe" (John 4:48).

Jesus obviously has no problem with signs and wonders and miracles. They followed His ministry everywhere and often. In fact, as you read on, you will see that He performed another healing right after His comment about the unbelief among the people.

But this time, the person's faith was on the word of God. A royal official's son was dying, and he requested that Jesus go to his son and heal him. Jesus said, "Go, your son lives." Then "the man believed the word that Jesus spoke and started off" (John 4:50). The man's son was healed at the time that he believed and acted on his faith.

Discouragement

God set a tremendous task before Nehemiah and His people. They were to rebuild the Jerusalem wall that had been destroyed. But when they saw the enormous amount of rubble, they were overwhelmed by it and became discouraged. Their faith waned. "Thus in Judah it was said, 'The strength of the burden-bearers is failing, yet there is much rubbish, and we ourselves are unable to rebuild the wall'" (Nehemiah 4:10).

They saw the pile of rubble as being bigger than God. When you get discouraged because of circumstances, you are seeing the circumstances as bigger than God. Your faith has been hindered. Discouragement is an instrument of your adversary and you must not give in to it.

Entanglement of Sin

"Therefore, since we have so great a cloud of witnesses surrounding us, let us also lay aside every encumbrance and the sin which so easily entangles us, and let us run with endurance the race that is set before us" (Hebrews 12:1).

Sin will entangle you and keep you from operating in the true spirit of faith. When you begin to develop overcoming, mountain-moving faith, your adversary will tempt you to enter into sin and to get you away from faith, which would defeat him.

Lack of Understanding and Insight

"My people are destroyed for lack of knowledge"

(Hosea 4:6a). Since faith must unite with, combine with, the word of God, not knowing what His word says hinders our faith.

We must know what God's word says and have the insight and discernment to know how to apply it to our lives. There is a song that says, "You can't stand on the promises if you don't know what they are." That is true. You cannot agree with God's word in faith, you cannot say, "Amen" to His word, if you do not know what it is.

"But My righteous one shall live by faith, and if he shrinks back, My soul has no pleasure in him. But we are not of those who shrink back to destruction, but of those who have faith to the preserving of the soul" (Hebrews 10:38-39).

We have looked at several things that will hinder our faith. Let us look at just a few more.

Situations that Appear Impossible

An entire chapter will be devoted to this later in the book.

Unbelieving Friends and Relatives

We read in the book of Mark, Chapter 5, verses 35-42, of an account in which the daughter of a synagogue official was sick to the point of death.

Jesus went to her house and found it filled with family

and friends who were loudly weeping and wailing. He walked in and told them the child had not died, she was only asleep. But they laughed at Jesus.

You need to know up front that if you are serious about developing overcoming, mountain-moving faith, it is likely you will have some friends and family who are not nearly as excited about it as you are. Some may mock you. Some may even laugh at you.

You may have to do what Jesus did: turn from them and do what God has called and anointed you to do. He turned from them and healed the little girl. He would not let their laughter hinder His faith. Do not let it hinder yours, either.

Scoffers

In reading the report as recorded in John 9:1-38, we learn of a blind man who Jesus healed. He was blind but now could see.

The scoffers were trying to discredit the healing. They claimed the man must not have really been blind. They said his sin caused his blindness. They said Jesus could not have healed him because it happened on the Sabbath, which made it a sin; so Jesus was a sinner, and a sinner could not have performed such a healing. And so it goes with scoffers. They will come up with one thing after another to deny a miracle.

Do not let scoffers hinder your faith. Do what God has called you to do and give Him all the glory as His power is displayed in and through you because of your faith.

Lack of Concern for the Hurting

A Canaanite woman cried out to Jesus to deliver her demon-possessed daughter. His disciples told Jesus, "Send her away, because she keeps shouting at us" (Matthew 15:23).

She asked Jesus for mercy, even though she was not "one of them." His reply was, "'O woman, your faith is great; it shall be done for you as you wish,' and her daughter was healed at once" (Matthew 15:28). Her faith was alive, active, expressed, and working. That is what counts with Jesus.

Love of Worldly Possessions

A rich young ruler came to Jesus asking what he needed to do to obtain eternal life. The man claimed he lived a good life according to the Ten Commandments, but he wanted to know what he was lacking.

"Jesus said to him, 'If you wish to be complete, go and sell your possessions and give to the poor and you will have treasure in heaven, and come follow Me'" (Matthew 19:21).

To keep the earthly treasures that he could see with his natural eyes, the young ruler turned down the heavenly treasures that could be seen only with the eyes of faith, and he walked away.

Opposition to the Truth

There are those who oppose the truth. They are "….always learning and never able to come to the knowledge of the truth. Just as Jannes and Jambres opposed Moses, so these men also opposed the truth, men of depraved mind, rejected in regard to the faith. But they will not make further progress, for their folly will be obvious to all, just as Jannes's and Jambres's folly was also" (2 Timothy 3:7-9).

One cannot oppose the truth of God's word and be in faith. "Sanctify them in the truth. Your word is truth" (John 17:17).

Other Hindrances

The above hindrances do not constitute a complete list. You can probably think of others, but hopefully you can now see that developing strong faith will not be accomplished without opposition. Endure in faith, and victory will be yours. You will become an overcomer, a mountain-mover, all to the glory of God!

Chapter 10

❖ ❖ ❖

Faith And The Impossible

A man came to Jesus, falling on his knees and saying, "Lord, have mercy on my son, for he is a lunatic and is very ill; for he often falls into the fire and often into the water. I brought him to Your disciples, and they could not cure him" (Matthew 17:15-16).

Jesus cast the demon out of the boy and the disciples came and asked why *they* could not help him. "Why could we not drive it out?"

And He said to them, "Because of the littleness of your faith; for truly I say to you, if you have faith the size of a mustard seed, you will say to this mountain, 'Move from here to there,' and it will move; and nothing will be impossible to you" (Matthew 17:19-20).

What the disciples needed when they were faced with an impossible situation was overcoming, mountain-moving faith.

How Can this Be?

When the angel came to Mary to announce that she would have a child and would call His name Jesus, it appeared to be an impossible situation. She was a virgin.

"Mary said to the angel, 'How can this be, since I am a virgin?'" (Luke 1:34). The angel replied, "Nothing will be impossible with God" (Luke 1:37).

Mary then essentially said, "Amen." Her recorded words were, "Behold, the bondslave of the Lord; may it be done to me according to Your word" (Luke 1:38). By faith, she put herself in agreement with the word of God.

We know the results of that impossible situation. Our Savior was born of Mary in the fullness of time. The promise, the word of God, was manifested in and through Mary in response to her faith.

When David faced Goliath everyone thought it was an impossible situation. The men were hiding in fear, David was but a shepherd boy, not a warrior, and the giant was huge.

Goliath had a spear and a sword. All David had was a sling and some smooth stones. But he also had faith. You know the rest of that story.

Without Becoming Weak in Faith

God spoke to Abraham and told him that He would make him the father of many nations. This looked like an impossible situation.

"In hope against hope he believed, so that he might become a father of many nations according to that which had been spoken, 'So shall your descendants be.' Without becoming weak in faith he contemplated his own body, now as good as dead since he was about a hundred years old, and the deadness of Sarah's womb; yet, with respect to the promise of God, he did not waver in unbelief but grew strong in faith, giving glory to God; and being fully assured that what God had promised, He was able also to perform" (Romans 4:18-21).

Abraham did not deny what he saw in the natural. He did wonder about it. But he chose to walk by faith, not by sight. He was unwavering in his faith in spite of the circumstances, all of which seemed to be in opposition to what God had promised. What an example for us today!

When faced with an impossible situation, Elisha relied on the word of God and the eyes of faith. He prayed that God would show his servant what *he* could see by faith. His faith brought victory. Read it in 2 Kings 6:8-17.

An Impossible Situation

When Moses was leading the people out of captivity, he faced an open sea. Behind him he could hear the rumble of chariots belonging to Pharaoh, who had changed his mind about letting the people go and had sent out his army to kill them all.

The sea on one side; a determined army on the other. An

impossible situation. God asked Moses what he had at hand, and Moses replied that all he had was a walking stick. God told him to use what he had, do what he could do, and raise the stick in the air. Moses obeyed in faith. Then God did the rest.

Moses had a word from God that he was to deliver His people, and he put his faith on that word, depending on God to work it all out. As the sea was parted, all God's people crossed over on dry land; and when the enemy army tried to come through, the water came back and drowned the whole bunch of them! Read the exciting account in the 14th chapter of the book of Exodus.

The Bible is filled with people facing impossible situations. Yet when they stayed in faith, God's word was manifested in and through them.

Using What You Have

Samson was captured and bound with two new ropes. "When he came to Lehi, the Philistines shouted as they met him. And the Spirit of the Lord came upon him mightily so that the ropes that were on his arms were as flax that is burned with fire, and his bonds dropped from his hands. He found a fresh jawbone of a donkey, so he reached out and took it and killed a thousand men with it" (Judges 15:14-15).

All Moses had was a walking stick; all Samson had was the jawbone of a donkey. But they both had faith in a mighty God who would save them in situations that looked impossible.

What are you facing that seems impossible? Can you find encouragement and strength to continue on in faith as you read how time after time God has honored faith?

Determined Faith

He will help you as surely as He did the woman who had suffered for years at the hand of doctors, spent all she had, yet only grew worse. An impossible situation. She had a hemorrhage for twelve years.

Then, "after hearing about Jesus, she came up in the crowd behind Him and touched His cloak. For she thought, 'If I just touch His garments, I will get well.' Immediately the flow of her blood was dried up; and she felt in her body that she was healed of her affliction" (Mark 5:27-29). Jesus then said to her, "Daughter, your faith has made you well; go in peace and be healed of your affliction" (Mark 5:34).

Since she had been sick for twelve years, her situation surely appeared beyond help. But when she heard of Jesus and put her faith in Him, everything changed.

Other Impossible Situations Overcome

Surely Jonah must have thought he had gotten into an impossible situation when he was in the belly of the large fish. Yet, through faith and thanksgiving, God delivered Him and brought him victory.

Elijah by himself faced 850 false prophets to determine whose god is God. All he had was a word from the Lord, but by faith he obtained the victory. See 1 Kings 18:20-39.

The man with the withered hand faced an impossible situation, yet when he responded to Jesus' words he found healing and new life. See Matthew 12:9-13.

Lame men walked again, deaf men heard again, blind men regained their sight, and mute men could speak, when they put their faith in Jesus and in the word of God.

There will be a chapter later on faith and healing, but I want you to see here that the Bible has multitudes of accounts of faith working in the most difficult of circumstances.

Which is Bigger?

What are your circumstances? Are you seeing them as greater than God? Or can you now see that His name is above all names and His power is unlimited, and with Him all things are possible?

Time after time, generation after generation, God has shown Himself faithful in turning impossible situations around for people when they put their trust and confidence in Him and allowed Him to take what they had to use as He would.

Let faith rise up in your spirit to lay hold of the word of the Lord. Agree with what He says and release His power and promises into your life!

Join with Jeremiah in saying, "Ah, Lord God! Behold, You have made the heavens and the earth by Your great power and by Your outstretched arm! Nothing is too difficult for You" (Jeremiah 32:17).

Do not be discouraged when faced with circumstances that look bleak all around. Know that the Lord is with you and He will respond to your faith when it is based on His word. Do not let your adversary steal your joy and peace and distract you from faith.

Fulfilling your Destiny with Faith

What dreams have you let die because they looked impossible? What has God spoken to you that may never be, because you would not endure in faith, but succumbed to the low life of walking by sight?

What work did God want to work in and through you but will never be able to do, because He had to choose someone else who would trust Him in what looked impossible?

As you develop and exercise your faith, it will become more and more like overcoming, mountain-moving faith and you will see things much differently. As your faith is ever enlarged, so will be your view of God and what He can do on your behalf to help you fulfill your destiny in Him.

Do not shun or avoid situations that look impossible. They can be opportunities for you to grow your faith stronger, experience God's faithfulness, and build a testimony to the validity and authenticity of God's word.

"Consider it all joy, my brethren, when you encounter various trials, knowing that the testing of your faith produces endurance. And let endurance have its perfect result, so that you may be perfect and complete, lacking in nothing" (James 1:2-4).

Chapter 11

❖ ❖ ❖

Signs And Wonders And Faith

"Everyone kept feeling a sense of awe; and many *wonders and signs* were taking place through the apostles" (Acts 2:43).

"The word of God kept on spreading and the number of the disciples continued to increase greatly in Jerusalem, and a great many of the priests were becoming obedient to the faith. And Stephen, full of grace and power, was performing great *wonders and signs* among the people" (Acts 6:7-8).

"Therefore they spent a long time there speaking boldly, with reliance upon the Lord, who was testifying to the word of His grace, granting that *signs and wonders* be done at their hands" (Acts 14:3).

"All the people kept silent, and they were listening to Barnabas and Paul as they were relating what *signs and wonders* God had done through them among the Gentiles" (Acts 15:12).

Signs that Follow Believers Who Walk in Faith

"'These signs will accompany those who have believed: in My name they will cast out demons, they will speak with new tongues, they will pick up serpents, and if they drink any deadly thing it will not hurt them; they will lay hands on the sick and they will recover. So then, when the Lord Jesus had spoken to them, He was received up into heaven and sat down at the right hand of God. And they went out and preached everywhere, while the Lord worked with them, and confirmed the word by the signs that followed" (Mark 16:17-20).

We often refer to the book that follows the four Gospels as the book of Acts. More properly it should be, "The Acts of the Apostles." That spells out more clearly that this book is about the acts or deeds of the Christ-followers of that time after they had received the mighty Baptism in the Holy Spirit.

Note a common thread in the Scripture passages quoted above. Signs and wonders were "performed" by the believers, they occurred "at their hands," but it was the Holy Spirit of God who was moving powerfully through them and made it all possible.

The verses from Mark are preceded by this: "Go into all the world and preach the Gospel to all creation" (Mark 16:15).

The charge by Jesus was to preach the Gospel, preach the Kingdom, preach the word of God; and if they would do so by faith, He would confirm or validate that word with supernatural signs and wonders.

They spent time preaching the word *with reliance on the Lord,* and the Lord was *testifying to that word with signs and wonders.* As the believers preached the word, signs accompanied them.

When they preached the word of healing, the Lord healed people through them. As they preached forgiveness, the Lord convicted people of the need to forgive. As they preached deliverance, they cast out demons in accordance to the word preached and the power of the Holy Spirit within them.

God's Confirmation of His Word

Signs and wonders are God's testimony or witness regarding His word. He is showing how the word works in those who believe. Signs and wonders verify or authenticate the word as absolute and unchanging truth.

Paul said this to the believers at Rome: "Therefore in Christ Jesus I have found reason for boasting in things pertaining to God. For I will not presume to speak of anything except what Christ has accomplished through me, resulting in the obedience of the Gentiles by word and deed, in the power of signs and wonders, in the power of the Spirit, so that from Jerusalem and round about as far as Illyricum I have fully preached the gospel" (Romans 15:17-19).

Paul said he could boast in what the Lord had done through him because as he preached the Gospel, he preached it fully. To fully preach the Gospel is to preach it in the power of the Holy Spirit with accompanying supernatural signs and wonders to confirm the word proclaimed.

"...God also testifying with them, both by signs and wonders and by various miracles and gifts of the Holy Spirit according to His own will" (Hebrews 2:4). It is God's will that signs and wonders would be performed at the hands of believers who proclaim His word with reliance on Him, in faith.

It is exciting to see how God moved through people in days gone by. It is even more exciting to read, "Jesus Christ is the same yesterday, and today, and forever" (Hebrews 13:8). You should expect signs and wonders to accompany the word of God that you proclaim in faith!

It Continues On

He still performs signs and wonders today through "those who believe."

Before empowering His followers, Jesus Himself performed many signs, wonders, and miracles. Lazarus was sick to the point of death. We read in John, Chapter 11, that they sent for Jesus to come. He waited a few days before He went. By the time He got there, Lazarus had died and had been buried in a tomb for four days.

Jesus called Lazarus out of death and out of the tomb. "Lazarus, come forth," He commanded. Then He told the people, "Unbind him, and let him go." But just before calling

Lazarus forth He said to those gathered there, "Did I not say to you that if you believe, you will see the glory of God?" (John 11:40).

Why did He say that? The same reason He said everything that He spoke, "...I do not speak on My own initiative, but by the Father abiding in Me" (John 14:10). Jesus said that He only spoke what He heard the Father speak. So in speaking to the people gathered at Lazarus' tomb, He was speaking the word of God. Then God confirmed that word by having Jesus call Lazarus forth.

God Reveals Himself Through Signs and Wonders

Signs and wonders encourage people to accept God's word as truth. They display the integrity of His unchanging word and unchanging character. It might be said that signs and wonders are God's signature verifying the authority of His word.

It should be noted here that the signs that were to accompany the preaching of the word were for "those who believe." When speaking of "preaching" the word, it is not implied that one has to occupy a pulpit ministry or any other specific office of ministry. To "preach" simply means to "proclaim." That applies to any believer who speaks the word of God or shares the word with others.

A key is that the word is to be spoken in faith, believing what God has said. God's word is a gift of grace that we receive by faith and speak forth with full "assurance of things hoped for, conviction of what is not yet seen."

Signs and wonders are to be a part of a believer's life so they can draw others to Jesus and can demonstrate how the word of God manifests when it is received by faith.

Paul said to the believers at Corinth, "The signs of a true apostle were performed among you with all perseverance, by signs and wonders and miracles" (2 Corinthians 12:12).

It Takes Faith

Trusting in the Lord, relying on Him, and having faith in God's word will result in signs and wonders in *your* life as your faith is increasing. When signs occur, be sure to do what Paul did: boast in what the Lord is doing. Give Him all the glory! For it is "the word of God, which also performs its work in you who believe" (1 Thessalonians 1:13b).

When Jesus sent the twelve disciples out, He first deputized them, delegating His authority to them. "Jesus summoned His twelve disciples and gave them authority over unclean spirits, to cast them out and to heal every kind of disease and every kind of sickness" (Matthew 10:1).

His instructions to them included, "And as you go, preach, saying, 'The kingdom of God is at hand.' Heal the sick, raise the dead, cleanse the lepers, cast out demons" (Matthew 10:7-8). In other words, Jesus told them to go preach the Gospel and signs and wonders would accompany them.

When sending out the seventy that He appointed to go before Him into the cities, His instructions included, "...and heal those in it who are sick, and say to them, 'The kingdom of God has come near you'" (Luke 10:9).

When they returned they were rejoicing, saying, "Lord, even the demons are subject to us in Your name" (Luke 10:17).

"These signs will accompany those who have believed: in My name..." "Jesus Christ is the same yesterday and today and forever" (Hebrews 13:8).

Step out in faith, believing. Allow the Lord to use you as one of His instruments through which He can perform signs and wonders, bringing healing, deliverance, and wholeness to people as you share His word in faith.

Chapter 12

❖ ❖ ❖

Faith And Thanksgiving

"Vindicate me, O Lord, for I have walked in my integrity, and I have trusted in the Lord without wavering. Examine me, O Lord, and try me; test my mind and my heart. For Your lovingkindness is before my eyes, and I have walked in Your truth. I do not sit with deceitful men, nor will I go with pretenders. I hate the assembly of evil doers, and I will not sit with the wicked. I shall wash my hands in innocence and I will go about Your altar, O Lord, that I may proclaim with the voice of thanksgiving and declare all Your wonders" (Psalm 26:1-7).

The psalmist here is testifying to his unwavering faith and trust in the Lord. He invites the Lord to test his faith and integrity, to the end that he might proclaim the wondrous works of God, with thanksgiving.

Thanksgiving and faith are closely tied together. When one expresses his assurance that God's word will be manifested just as God has said it would be, his heart is filled with thanksgiving. It might be said that thanksgiving is in fact an expression of faith when one shows gratitude even for things not yet seen, not yet manifested.

Exalting the Lord with Faith

"O come, let us sing for joy to the Lord, let us shout joyfully to the rock of our salvation. Let us come before His presence with thanksgiving; let us shout joyfully to Him with psalms. For the Lord is a great God, and a great King above all gods, in whose hand are the depths of the earth; the peaks of the mountains are His also.

"The sea is His, for it was He who made it, and His hands formed the dry land. Come, let us worship and bow down, let us kneel before the Lord our Maker. For He is our God, and we are the people of His pasture and the sheep of His hand" (Psalm 95:1-7).

The psalmist is telling of coming before God's presence with thanksgiving and joy, worshiping Him for all His power and majesty. When we magnify and exalt God and see how big and powerful He is, it is easier to believe He is able to perform His word.

The Overflow of Gratitude from Faith

"Therefore as you have received Christ Jesus the Lord, so walk in Him, having been firmly rooted and now being built up in Him and established in your faith, just as you were instructed, and overflowing with gratitude" (Colossians 2:6-

7). As we are established firmly in faith, our hearts overflow with thanksgiving.

Thanksgiving pleases God because it is an expression of faith and an acknowledgment that it is He who performs His work in those who believe, and not us.

Jonah was called by God to take a prophetic word to Nineveh. But Jonah ran from the call and ended up in the belly of a large fish. He was in a terrible mess.

"Water encompassed me to the point of death. The great deep engulfed me. Weeds were wrapped around my head. I descended to the roots of the mountains. The earth with its bars was around me forever..." (Jonah 2:5-6).

When Jonah's thoughts and focus turned from his miserable circumstances to the Lord and His faithfulness, things began to change. "But I will sacrifice to You with the voice of thanksgiving that which I have vowed I will pay. Salvation is from the Lord" (Jonah 2:9).

When he was fainting away, he remembered the Lord. See verse seven.

Jonah's thinking back on God's faithfulness created a heart of thanksgiving for what He had done and stirred up faith for his deliverance. "Then the Lord commanded the fish, and it vomited Jonah up onto the dry land" (Jonah 2:10).

Our Testimony Brings forth Thanksgiving

When we recall the marvelous ways the Lord has worked

in our lives, we realize that He will also bring us through our present situation.

When facing Goliath, David remembered with gratitude how the Lord had already delivered him from a bear and a lion. That gave him courage and faith that God would help him in his current need as he faced the giant.

As we thank God for all He has already done in our lives, we can also thank Him for His promises that are yet to come, knowing by faith they *will* come forth. God is faithful. "...for He who promised is faithful" (Hebrews 10:23).

Take Care of What You Have Before Asking for More

While waiting on promises not yet manifested, we should demonstrate our gratitude for what we already have. That is done by exhibiting good stewardship. When we declare that every good and perfect gift comes down from the Father above, and we realize everything belongs to Him, we will take better care of what He shares with us to have and to use.

Do not set your heart on a better car if you are not taking care of the one you have. Do not ask for a larger house if the one you have is in disrepair. Do not pray for your children to be better behaved, if you have not been diligent in training them up in the ways of the Lord.

If we are really grateful for something, we will take care of it and provide proper maintenance for it. If you appreciate your marriage, you will continually work at it and watch over it diligently. You will continue to learn how to make it an even more fulfilling relationship. The same is true with your faith.

Faith and Thanksgiving Bring Forth Victory

It is God's will that we be grateful. "In everything give thanks, for this is God's will for you in Christ Jesus" (1 Thessalonians 5:18).

Paul declared, "Thanks be to God, who always leads us in triumph in Christ, and manifests through us the sweet aroma of the knowledge of Him in every place" (2 Corinthians 2:14). At another time he said, "but thanks be to God, who gives us the victory through our Lord Jesus Christ" (1 Corinthians 15:57).

As Paul lived by faith, he was faced with circumstances worse than most will ever face. Yet he walked by faith and not by sight. As he continually looked at every situation through the eyes of faith, he was fully assured of the triumph and victory that was on its way, in Christ Jesus.

What released the miracle of feeding the multitude with a few small fish and loaves of bread? It was that Jesus expressed His faith by holding up to Heaven and blessing what they had. He knew His Heavenly Father would come through with an appropriate provision, or else He would not have had the people sit down to eat.

As we go to God to receive His promises and provisions

by faith, it is to be done with thanksgiving. "Be anxious for nothing, but in everything by prayer and supplication with thanksgiving let your requests be made known to God. And the peace of God, which surpasses all comprehension, will guard your hearts and your minds" (Philippians 4:6 -7).

"Devote yourselves to prayer, keeping alert in it with an attitude of thanksgiving" (Colossians 4:2).

Turning to God in faith and receiving the blessings He has stored up for us will lead to a life of thanksgiving and praise.

Chapter 13

❖ ❖ ❖

Faith And Healing

You have undoubtedly heard someone say, and perhaps you have said it yourself: "Well, I don't believe in that faith healing stuff."

Jesus did believe in faith healing. In the Scriptures, healing is nearly always connected directly to faith. As He physically walked on earth, Jesus spent a great deal of His time healing people in response to their faith. Read the Gospels carefully and see for yourself. A number of passages will be included in this chapter.

When some say they do not believe in faith healing it is because they have seen some charlatan add to or pervert the Scriptures and claim a healing ministry. Remember, there is no such thing as a counterfeit three-dollar bill. In order for there to be a counterfeit, there has to be a real three-dollar bill. Do not let a counterfeit keep you from the real thing! Put your faith in God and His word alone. Let us look at some examples from His word.

Jesus the Healer

"When Jesus came down from the mountain, large crowds followed Him. And a leper came to Him and bowed down before Him, and said, 'Lord, if You are willing, You can make me clean.' Jesus stretched out His hand and touched him, saying, 'I am willing; be cleansed.' And immediately his leprosy was cleansed" (Matthew 8:1-3).

One of the first things one must settle regarding healing is whether or not it is God's will to heal. Jesus clearly stated here that He is willing. It is His will to heal. Based on that word, the leper, by faith, received his healing.

The Bible is explicitly clear about healing being God's will. Consider the following: Jesus said He only said what the Father was saying and He only did what the Father was showing Him to do. If He healed someone, it was because God was telling Him to. God would not ask Jesus to do something against His will.

When God created all things, including man, He looked at His creation and declared that all was good. He could not have looked upon sickness and disease and said that it was good.

God did not create sickness; it came with the fall of man in the Garden as Adam and Eve rebelled against God's word and Satan brought all manner of corruption into the creation. Thorns and thistles, disease and sickness, all were a part of the corruption. So was sin.

Jesus went about doing good and healing every kind of

sickness and every kind of disease. "The Son of God appeared for this purpose, to destroy the works of the devil" (1 John 3:8b).

"You know of Jesus of Nazareth, how God anointed Him with the Holy Spirit and with power, and how He went about doing good and healing all who were oppressed by the devil, for God was with Him" (Acts 10:38).

If you believe it is the will of God that you be sick or diseased, then surely you would not seek any form of medical help or relief, because that would be opposing God's will for you. But it is God's will that His people are healed and whole.

Understanding Authority and Faith

"And when Jesus entered Capernaum, a centurion came to Him, imploring Him, and saying, 'Lord, my servant is lying paralyzed at home, fearfully tormented.' Jesus said to him, 'I will come and heal him.' But the centurion said, 'Lord, I am not worthy for You to come under my roof, but just say the word, and my servant will be healed. For I also am a man under authority, with soldiers under me; and I say to this one, "Go!" and he goes, and to another, "Come!" and he comes, and to my slave, "Do this!" and he does it.' Now when Jesus heard this, He marveled and said to those who were following, 'Truly I say to you, I have not found such great faith with anyone in Israel'" (Matthew 8:5-10).

The centurion understood the power that is released

when one with legitimate authority speaks. Recognizing the authority Jesus had, he said to Him, "Just say the word and my servant will be healed." Not might be, not may be, but he *will* be healed. The centurion put his faith on the word of God that Jesus spoke. Remember, our faith, like the centurion's, has to be on the authority of God's unchangeable word.

Jesus Fulfills Prophecy of Healing

"When evening came, they brought to Him many who were demon-possessed; and He cast out the spirits with a word, and healed all who were ill. This was to fulfill what was spoken through Isaiah the prophet: 'He Himself took our infirmities and carried away our diseases'" (Matthew 8:16-17).

Jesus was fulfilling the word of God that had been prophesied by Isaiah many years before. It was that word which was the basis for Jesus to heal.

Forgiveness and Faith

"Getting into a boat, Jesus crossed over the sea and came to His own city. And they brought to Him a paralytic lying on a bed. Seeing their faith, Jesus said to the paralytic, 'Take courage, son; your sins are forgiven'" (Matthew 9:1-2). Jesus discerned the faith of the people who brought the lame man to him, and He responded to it.

Recognizing that the on-lookers were thinking evil thoughts about Jesus having pronounced forgiveness to the man, He said to them, "Which is easier, to say, 'Your sins are forgiven' or to say, 'Get up, and walk'? But so that you may know that the Son of Man has authority on earth to forgive sins, He then said to the paralytic, 'Get up, pick up your bed and go home.' And he got up and went home."

Healing and forgiveness are often spoken of together in the Scriptures. "He pardons all your iniquities, He heals all your diseases..." (Psalm 103:3).

Your Faith has Made You Well

"And a woman who had been suffering from a hemorrhage for twelve years came up behind Him and touched the fringe of His cloak; for she was saying to herself, 'If I only touch His garment, I will get well.' But Jesus, turning and seeing her, said, 'Daughter, take courage; your faith has made you well.' At once the woman was made well." Notice that Jesus said it was her faith that brought forth her healing. She said, "I *will* get well." Faith is the *assurance* of things hoped for, the *conviction* of things not yet seen.

Agreeing With Jesus

"As Jesus went on from there, two blind men followed Him crying out, 'Have mercy on us, Son of David!' When He entered the house, the blind men came up to Him, and Jesus said to them, 'Do you believe that I am able to do this?' They said to Him, 'Yes, Lord.' Then He touched their eyes, saying, 'It shall be done to you according to your faith.' And their eyes were opened...' (Matthew 9:27-30a).

Are you beginning to see how Jesus responds to faith? Faith in the word of God brings forth its manifestation. His word performs its work in those who believe.

His Healing Ministry

"Jesus was going through all the cities and villages, teaching in their synagogues and proclaiming the gospel of the kingdom, and healing every kind of disease and every kind of sickness" (Matthew 9:35). Would this be a good place to remind ourselves that "Jesus Christ is the same yesterday, and today, and forever"? (Hebrews 13:8). Every kind of sickness, every kind of disease was and still can be healed by Jesus!

"And when the men of that place recognized Him, they sent word into that entire surrounding district and brought to Him all who were sick; and they implored Him that they might just touch the fringe of His cloak. And as many as touched it were cured" (Matthew 14:35-36).

Great Faith

Let us look at just a few more specific cases of healing. A Canaanite woman came to Jesus asking Him to help her daughter who was "cruelly demon-possessed." See Matthew 15:22. The disciples were imploring Jesus to send the woman away. She was being bothersome. But the woman persisted, and Jesus, seeing her tenacity, said to her, "O woman, your faith is great; it shall be done for you as you wish.' And her daughter was healed at once." (Matthew 15:28).

This was simply different wording than what Jesus often said: "Be it done according to your faith." Jesus responds to faith, and He said of this woman who was persistent in faith, that her faith was "great." The result was healing.

Bringing Glory to God

"Departing from there, Jesus went along by the Sea of Galilee, and having gone up on the mountain, He was sitting there. And large crowds came to Him, bringing with them those who were lame, crippled, blind, mute, and many others, and they laid them down at His feet; and He healed them. So the crowd marveled as they saw the mute speaking, the crippled restored, the lame walking, and the blind seeing; and they glorified the God of Israel" (Matthew 15:29-31). God is glorified when people acknowledge Him as who He says He is, the God that heals.

Littleness of Faith

A man brought his son, an epileptic, to the disciples of Jesus. His seizures caused the boy to become very ill, often falling into the fire or into the water. A demon was causing the seizures. The disciples could not cast the demon out, so they asked Jesus why they were ineffective in bringing deliverance to the boy.

Jesus replied, "Because of the littleness of your faith; for truly I say to you, if you have faith the size of a mustard seed, you will say to this mountain, 'Move from here to there,' and it will move; and nothing will be impossible to you" (Matthew

17:20). The disciples still had some developing to do in the area of faith. Do we not also? Or, have you already achieved overcoming, mountain-moving faith? If not, read on.

Jesus called the generation of His time an "unbelieving generation," a generation with little faith. What does He say about our generation?

Basis for Your Belief

Whether or not you believe in faith and healing, Jesus has made it clear what *He* thinks about it.

Do not let man-made traditions of any church or denomination, or any teaching based on unbelief, be your basis for faith when it comes to healing. Faith must be based on the word of God, and that alone.

"Surely our sickness He Himself bore, and our sorrows He carried; yet we ourselves esteemed Him stricken, smitten of God, and afflicted. But He was pierced through for our transgressions, He was crushed for our iniquities; the chastening for our well-being fell upon Him, and by His scourging we are healed" (Isaiah 53:4-5).

"And He Himself bore our sins in His body on the cross, so that we might die to sin and live to righteousness; for by His wounds you were healed" (1 Peter 2:24).

An Example of Tradition

There are three ways to determine the meaning of something:

1. Look up the definition in a dictionary.

2. Determine the meaning from the context.

3. See how it is used elsewhere.

In biblical matters we have a fourth way:

4. See how it fits with the nature and character of God

There is not enough space here to look at all the traditions that man has established which are not in accordance with the truth of Scripture, so we will look at only one example by way of illustration.

In reference to 2 Corinthians 12:7-10, the tradition of some churches has been to say that Paul was sick, that he asked God three times to heal him, and God said, "No, I'm not going to heal you. My grace is all you need."

All four of the ways of determining the meaning of something can be applied.

The "thorn in the flesh," Paul says, "is a messenger from Satan." The word "messenger" is "angelos" in the original Greek language of the New Testament. It is pronounced, "ang'-e-los." You can see where the word "angel" comes from.

Angelos is used many times in the Bible, and it *always* refers to a personality, never to a disease. It always means a messenger and may refer to a holy angel of God, angels or messengers of the devil (demons), or even to men such as prophets or pastors who are messengers.

The word "thorn" is used elsewhere in Scripture. See Numbers 33:55, Joshua 23:13, 2 Samuel 23:6, and Judges 2:2-3. In all cases, "thorns" refer to people.

Paul said this messenger of Satan buffeted him. To buffet is to strike blow after blow, like waves pounding on a ship at sea.

Paul was buffeted by "thorns in the flesh" wherever he went, and the people that resisted him and his message were carrying out the work of the devil to try to shut Paul's ministry down, to silence his message of the gospel.

Today we would call such people a "pain in the neck," which would essentially mean the same as a "thorn in the flesh."

Did God say no to Paul's request to remove such problematic and bothersome people who were coming against him? God's answer was better than what Paul asked for. Rather than removing the resistance, God reminded Paul that He had the authority to overcome such nuisances because of the power of God's grace working in and through him. Paul then could teach believers: "But in all these things we overwhelmingly conquer through Him who loved us" (Romans 8:37).

Paul received an understanding of what would be recorded for all time: "Greater is He [Jesus] that is in you, than he [the devil] that is in the world" (1 John 4:4). God was telling him what God spoke through James, "[You] resist the devil and he will flee from you" (James 4:7).

Paul realized that in his own strength, he was powerless; but in Christ, with God's power, he had authority over the devil and his messengers and could "tread upon serpents and scorpions" and defeat the devil himself! It is the same with Christ-followers today!

Can you see why the devil would rather have people believe and teach that Paul was sick and God would not heal him, so we would not expect to be healed today?

Develop your belief system and your doctrine of healing and faith based on the word of God, not on the traditions of man!

Chapter 14

❖ ❖ ❖

Contending Earnestly For The Faith

The book of Jude was written by Jude, brother of James, half-brother of Jesus, between 60 and 80 A.D. His purpose in writing was to confront the problems of false teachers and false doctrine that were hindering, distorting, and destroying the believers' faith.

Even today, his words are a reminder of the need for constant vigilance by believers not to compromise the word of God or draw back from it. "Beloved, while I was making every effort to write to you about our common salvation, I felt the necessity to write to you appealing that you contend earnestly for the faith which was once for all handed down to the saints" (Jude 3).

Jude was exhorting the believers to fight for the faith which they had. Not just to fight for it, but to *earnestly* fight for it. Encouraging them to be faithful to Christ, he instructed them to hold on to what they had obtained and to hold on with intensity, tenacity, and purpose.

The Good Fight of Faith

Paul similarly wrote to the believers at Philippi, "Only conduct yourselves in a manner worthy of the gospel of Christ, so that whether I come and see you or remain absent, I will hear of you that you are standing firm in one spirit, with one mind striving together for the faith of the gospel..." (Philippians 1:27).

To contend is to stand firm and fight. Jude and Paul were encouraging believers to stand firm in faith. Stand firm on the unchangeable word of God. Fight for truth. Defend the Lord and His word that you rely on.

"This command I entrust to you, Timothy, my son, in accordance with the prophecies previously made concerning you, that by them you fight the good fight, keeping faith and a good conscience, which some have rejected and suffered shipwreck in regard to their faith" (1 Timothy 1:18-19).

"Fight the good fight of faith..." (1 Timothy 6:12a).

When one begins to develop his faith, a battle will ensue. There will be other people and even circumstances that will speak out against the very word of God which we have learned to receive by faith. To contend is literally to fight a fight as a combatant. We are to exert ourselves to the utmost in defense of God's word and our faith, even when it seems costly. It may mean taking a stand even against those in the churches if they deny the power of God and the authority of His word.

Faith Never Compromises

We just read that Paul spoke of those who have rejected faith, or who had faith and it became shipwrecked.

"But the Spirit explicitly says that in later times some will fall away from the faith, paying attention to deceitful spirits and doctrines of demons..." (1 Timothy 4:1). Falling away implies they once had faith, but lost it.

Walking in faith, living in faith, is not something that we start and then just put on cruise control. We must carefully watch over our faith, develop it to become ever stronger, and steadfastly resist any effort to compromise, diminish, or destroy it.

We must contend earnestly for our faith. Those in faith must never allow God's word to be compromised in its authority, or distorted in its truth, or explained away regarding its power and promises.

"But realize this, that in the last days difficult times will come. For men will be lovers of self, lovers of money, boastful, arrogant, revilers, disobedient to parents, ungrateful, unholy, unloving, irreconcilable, malicious gossips, without self-control, brutal, haters of good, treacherous, reckless, conceited, lovers of pleasure rather than lovers of God, holding to a form of godliness, although they have denied its power. Avoid such men as these" (2 Timothy 3:1-5).

Isaiah prophesied long ago of these days: "Then the Lord said, '... this people draw near with their words and honor Me with their lip service, but they remove their hearts far from Me, and their reverence for Me consists of tradition learned by rote'" (Isaiah 29:13).

Tradition is Not the Basis for Faith

Jesus spoke to a group of just such people: the Pharisees and scribes. "And He answered and said to them, 'Why do you yourselves transgress the commandment of God for the sake of your tradition?'" (Matthew 15:3). Then He quoted Isaiah's prophecy, "You hypocrites, rightly did Isaiah prophesy of you: 'this people honors Me with their lips, but their heart is far away from Me. But in vain do they worship Me, teaching as doctrines the precepts of men'" (Matthew 15:7-9).

There are people today who go to church, hold to the traditions of their denomination, obey all the rules of the church, and yet deny the truth and power of God's word. They are not living by faith. You cannot live by faith if you do not believe God's word is true, because you have no basis for your faith.

"All Scripture is inspired by God and profitable for teaching, for reproof, for correction, for training in righteousness; so that the man of God may be adequate, equipped for every good work" (2 Timothy 3:16). All means *all*. All Scripture is inspired by God.

"The grass withers, the flower fades, but the word of our God stands forever" (Isaiah 40:8). The unchanging word of God is the basis for our faith. Do not let others tell you differently.

We must contend for our faith without distorting it,

without trying to adapt the word to fit our circumstances. We are to adapt our circumstances to the word of God.

As we have seen, Scripture clearly tells us that not all who start out in faith end in faith. Some will fall away; some will be shipwrecked in their faith. And some will lightly esteem their faith, thus rendering it ineffective.

Circumstances will cause some to compromise their faith saying, "Well, so-and-so really loved God and was not healed, so God must just heal some, not others. It must not be His will to heal everyone." Is that what the word of God says?

Faith does Not Shrink Back

"Jesus was going through all the cities and villages, teaching in their synagogues and proclaiming the gospel of the kingdom, and healing every kind of disease and every kind of sickness" (Matthew 9:35). "Jesus Christ is the same yesterday and today and forever" (Hebrews 13:8).

We must not pull back in these days from proclaiming *all* of God's word, as it is written.

"Every word of God is tested; He is a shield to those who take refuge in Him. Do not add to His words or He will reprove you, and you will be proved a liar" (Proverbs 30:5-6).

Remember how we add to God's word, usually by interjecting a conjunction, when we say something like, "Yes,

I know the word of God says He will forgive all our sins and heal all our diseases, *but*..." Remember, whatever you say after "but" will deny or negate your belief in the word of God.

"I know He is my comforter and the Prince of Peace; however..." When you add the conjunctions, whatever follows shows that you are not assured of the truth and power of God's word. Do not add to His word because of the sake of your tradition or what your friends might say that contradicts His word. That is what Paul called "shrinking" back.

Paul said, "For I did not shrink from declaring to you the whole purpose of God" (Acts 20:27). Other versions say the whole "counsel" of God. We could even say he did not hold back from preaching the whole "word" of God.

Paul did not hold back by ceasing to preach the fullness of the word of God, even when faced with stiff opposition or circumstances that appeared contrary to the word.

"Do not throw away your confidence, which has a great reward" (Hebrews 10:35). When your confidence is in the Lord and in His word, you are in faith. Faith has a great reward.

What does God say about the one who draws back from faith? "But My righteous one shall live by faith, and if he shrinks back, My soul has no pleasure in him" (Hebrews 10:38). The writer of the book of Hebrews said, "But we are not of those who shrink back to destruction, but of those who have faith to the preserving of the soul" (Hebrews 10:39).

Stay Strong in Faith

As we contend earnestly with our enemies, the opponents of our faith, we must do so out of strength. We must keep strong in faith

Jude again has some sound advice. "But you, beloved, building yourselves up on your most holy faith, praying in the Holy Spirit..." (Jude 3).

Stay in the fight. Contend earnestly for your faith. As you face opposition to your development of overcoming, mountain-moving faith, stand strong and press on!

"For we have become partakers of Christ, if we hold fast the beginning of our assurance firm until the end..." (Hebrews 3:14).

Chapter 15

❖ ❖ ❖

Leaving A Legacy Of Faith

Legacy. Something that has been handed down from an ancestor or predecessor.

Our legacy is what we leave behind for those who follow after us. We often think of legacy as something we leave for our children upon our death, an inheritance. It is often thought of in terms of material possessions alone.

Some people work hard all their lives to accumulate wealth so they can leave behind houses, cars, stocks and other investments, and whatever else it takes to make life easier for their children after they themselves are gone. There is nothing wrong with wanting to bless your children. But there is something greater to leave than material possessions, and that is a legacy of faith. By instruction and example, we can leave our children a greater understanding of faith than that which we may have inherited.

We can also leave a legacy of faith to those beyond our own family, and the legacy can enter into effect even before we die. Seeing your integrity and passion for true overcoming, mountain-moving faith may draw others to a like desire to bring glory to God and to please Him with real, biblical faith.

As they see that you know what the promises and provisions of God are and watch as you receive them into your life, they will see how faith and the word of God work in and through human flesh. They will see that biblical faith is not just a philosophy or theory; it is a reality that God created.

As others see steadfastness and consistency in your reliance on the word of God and in your confidence in the Lord, they may be encouraged to "imitate those who by faith and patience inherit the promises."

Leaving a legacy of faith for others is far more valuable than whatever material possessions you may accumulate and leave behind.

May the Lord bless your endeavors to illustrate to others what faith is, so they may see and understand that, "Without faith it is impossible to please Him, for he who comes to God must believe that He is and that He is a rewarder of those who seek Him" (Hebrews 11:6).

"Let us hold fast the confession of our hope without wavering, for He who promised is faithful" (Hebrews 10:23).

"Now may the God of hope fill you with all joy and peace in believing, so that you will abound in hope by the power of the Holy Spirit" (Romans 15:13).

About the Author

Gary Ward has been pastor of Living Word Church in Manhattan, Kansas, since 1983.

He has a heart for helping people come to Christ and walk in the new life that He offers: A life free from the pains and heartaches of the past. A life of new promise and hope. A life that experiences the inheritance we have in the Lord. A life free of the shackles that hold us to our past. A life that releases us to live in the present in its fullness while looking to the future with great hope.

That is what his last book, "Living Free from the Shackles that Bind," is all about. Living that life of freedom requires strong and effective faith. That is what *this* book is about.

Before entering the ministry, Gary taught high school biology for 18 years and worked as a seasonal ranger for the National Park Service during the summers. During those years he wrote the booklet "Bears of the Great Smoky Mountains" as well as numerous articles for magazines.

Gary has become best known for his ability to preach the Bible in a very practical, easy to understand way and always with encouragement to apply the word of God and see it manifested in the lives of those who hear it.

Many signs and wonders have accompanied the preaching of the whole counsel of God and have attested to the power and practicality of God's word.

Gary's only desire in writing this book is that it reaches people with a message of what real Bible faith is: A faith that works. A faith that can be increasingly effective through use. A faith that brings the promises and provisions of God into reality in the believer's life. A faith that will lead to great joy and peace regardless of the circumstances that may surround us.

Need additional copies?

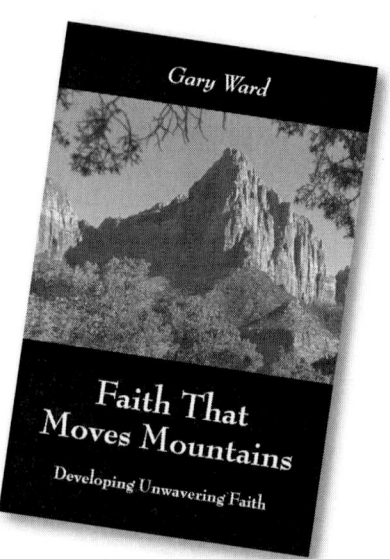

To order more copies of
Faith That Moves Mountains,
contact NewBookPublishing.com

- ❏ Order online at NewBookPublishing.com
- ❏ Call 877-311-5100 or
- ❏ Email Info@NewBookPublishing.com

Another book available by Gary Ward -
Living Free from the Shackles that Bind

Order your copies today!